Cooking Among Friends®

Meal Planning and Preparation Delightfully Simplified

Published by *Cooking Among Friends, LLC,* Allendale, Michigan
Typesetting: Exactgraphics and Holland Litho
Graphics and Page Design: Mike Mason and Exactgraphics

Publisher's Cataloging-in-Publication
(Provided by Quality Books, Inc.)

Tennant, Mary.
   Cooking among friends : meal planning and preparation
delightfully simplified / Mary Tennant, Becki Visser. --
1st ed.
   p. cm.
   LCCN: 2001118935
   ISBN: 0970156111 (paperback)

   1. Make-ahead cookery. 2. Quick and easy cookery.
I. Visser, Becki. II. Title.

TX652.T46 2001   641.5'55
                QBI01-201288

Acknowledgements

Celebrating

Bob
Jessica and Ashley

Randy
Mitchell, Macie, and Sierra

Contact Us

Cooking Among Friends, LLC welcomes your questions, comments, and suggestions. We'd love to hear from you!

Cooking Among Friends, LLC
P.O. Box 84
Allendale, Michigan 49401

616.895.6909

www.cookingamongfriends.com

mailbox@cookingamongfriends.com
mary@cookingamongfriends.com
becki@cookingamongfriends.com

Table of Contents

Chapter 5

Beyond Entrée Recipes 153

Chapter 6

Freezing—A Quick Review

Chapter 7

Resources

The Story Behind Cooking Among Friends®

We know the scene. It plays out every day. At the height of the late-afternoon's momentum, somewhere amid transitioning from work to home, collecting a mini-van full of soccer players or emptying backpacks, someone asks, "What's for dinner?" and our blood runs cold. Three little words that can send us into a mind-numbing, babbling search for coherence that often ends with, sigh, "How about take-out?" And somewhere, deep inside, we hear "cop-out."

Two years ago, I went on a mission. Like many of you, I began to simplify my life. Clutter began moving by the vanloads from my closets to the local Goodwill. With a new vision, I began to say "no" with increasing confidence to the activities that wanted to crowd my planner, and crowd out the good things for which I wanted to foster a time and place. I was intent on streamlining my daily activities so I could focus more time and energy on building the heart of my home. And at the top of my list was meal planning and preparation.

It was the beginning of *Cooking Among Friends*®. I gathered a group of five friends and we committed to do meal planning and preparation together. We first established the guidelines, food preferences, and food restrictions that would govern our group. We then established a menu of six entrées that each person was delighted to have in her freezer. We each chose an entrée to prepare in bulk and freeze in meal-sized portions (at least two meals for each group member). And then we got together to swap our meals, plan the next menu of entrées, and share a rejuvenating evening. We evaluated our meals to determine which ones were eligible for repetition and started a list of favorites that would become a resource when planning new menus.

My family meals are now served in a time warp. In a June Cleaver moment, meals are served with grace and ease. I'm able to greet my Ward feeling fresh and fabulous, not frantic and frazzled. My little Wally and Beaver sit down to a delicious, nutritious meal where, food preparation aside, I have energy remaining to focus on nourishing their spirits. Family dinnertime like it used to be.

And me? Well, on a regular basis I'm hanging out with the most incredible little group of women you could ever hope to find. We're sharing the journey. And we're working together to build the hearts of our homes with a great family mealtime. It just doesn't get any better than that.

Mary Tennant

Chapter 1

About Cooking Among Friends®

The Basics

Cooking Among Friends® suggests you gather a group of friends and commit to working together to do meal planning and preparation. As a group, you'll establish a menu of entrées pleasing to each member of the group. Each person will prepare one (or more) of the entrées in bulk and freeze it in meal-sized portions. The group will then get together for an exchange gathering where each member will trade for the other frozen entrées, establish the next menu of entrées, and determine when to meet again for the next exchange. You'll collaborate in advance to determine the following, and we'll coach you along the way!

- What size individually frozen entrée will define a "meal" for your group.
- How many individual meals, per person, will be prepared for each exchange.
- How frequently an exchange will occur.
- How financial equality will be maintained.
- What general guidelines, restrictions, and preferences will be standard for your group.

A Better Way

There is a better way to do family meal planning and preparation in your home. *Cooking Among Friends*® suggests you gather a group of friends, collaborate, plan a menu of entrées, individually prepare a large quantity of a single entrée (or two), freeze it in meal-sized portions, and then swap! We show you how. It's a way that works, and a way that brings incredible benefits.

Bask in peace of mind.

A freezer full of prepared entrées brings incredible peace of mind! Rest assured that no matter how hectic the day, or how empty the refrigerator and pantry, you'll be prepared to feed the family or entertain friends. You'll always have an available answer to the inevitable question, "What's for dinner?"

You'll also relish the peace and joy found in facilitating a great family mealtime. Having the evening meal prepared ahead makes it possible to significantly slow down the pace and soften the tone of your evenings. Not having to focus on what's for dinner allows you to focus on connecting with the ones you love.

Reclaim your time.

Cooking Among Friends® is a time saving proposition. Dividing the time you spend to prepare your entrée for exchange by the number of meals you produce is convincing. Other time savers may be less apparent. You will enjoy the luxury of scheduling a block of time to prepare your meals, choosing the date and time you will be most productive. You will do significantly less grocery shopping. Your meal planning efforts will be extremely efficient (and fun!). Nightly meal clean-up will be a breeze. And you'll find that meal preparation (reheating an entrée and tossing a salad) can easily be delegated to other members of the family.

Reduce your expenses.

Cooking Among Friends® is a money saving proposition. Preparing one recipe, in bulk, puts you in an optimal buying position. At last, you'll be able to take advantage of gallon-sized containers of sour cream or tomato sauce. Group members will be able to anticipate future exchanges and buy meat in bulk when prices are at their absolute lowest. Your group may decide to purchase and divide large quantities of staples like flour, sugar, rice, pasta, and spices.

We think you'll get savvy as never before. Working together as a group makes it fun. One of the members of our group scans weekly grocery store advertisements and alerts all the members to exceptional prices. Another member of the group maintains and shares a list of frequently used ingredients with price comparison between a local grocery store, bulk club, and restaurant supply store.

We think you'll save money with improved food management. With many of your meals prepared all at once, in advance, you will not juggle as many fresh food items. You'll throw away fewer pot roasts that never make it to the pot during a weekend-turned-hectic and chicken breasts that get buried under restaurant leftovers.

But perhaps best of all, with a freezer full of great food, you will no longer need to resort to expensive take-out meals. Save take-out, or dining out, for when it will be a pleasure instead of a begrudged necessity!

Build a circle of friends.

One of the truly great benefits of *Cooking Among Friends*® is building friendships. Unless we're fairly intentional about catching up with friends, sharing life with them can pass us by. *Cooking Among Friends*® has a built-in "catch up with friends" factor. You'll be in touch with a circle of friends on a regular basis. And you'll be supporting one another in a significant, meaningful way by working together to answer the question, "What's for dinner?"

Q&A's

Q Does the technique work for a variety of family structures and lifestyles?

A We find the technique works for just about anyone who would like to eat quality meals at home on a regular basis. Our group represents couples (no children) and families (varying in size from four members to five members). We have helped form groups that include singles, empty nesters, stay-at-home moms, single dads, working moms, and stay-at-home dads. The simplicity and flexibility of *Cooking Among Friends*® makes it widely appealing!

Singles can greatly benefit from *Cooking Among Friends*®. It puts them in a bulk buying position, and eliminates the "cooking for one" hassle. It allows for a freezer full of high quality, cost effective, individually-sized entrées of preference. And it allows for camaraderie among a group of culinary friends!

Cooking Among Friends® is also a wonderful solution when the person typically responsible for meal preparation travels or juggles many other responsibilities. It is very effective for the household where a dieter does not wish to impose the diet on the rest of the family. It may be a solution and a comfort for a household experiencing illness. If family members or friends could assist in preparing an entrée for exchange, the family would have prepared meals in the freezer for many days to come.

Q Would you suggest we prepare enough meals to last a month?

A We suggest you work together as a group to answer this question. See our form *Establishing Group Guidelines*. This form will walk you through defining the objectives and parameters that will govern your group.

Our group exchanges twelve to eighteen meals on a monthly basis. (Twelve meals is our minimum commitment. But recipes vary in cost to prepare. If our predetermined budgetary figure will allow for eighteen meals, we are obligated to provide the additional meals.) While this may not sound adequate to cover a month's worth of days, we have found it to be appropriate for our group. It allows for flexibility to occasionally cook something we're craving (which usually adds a few more meals to the frozen stash), dine out, eat leftovers, go on vacation, or experiment with new recipes to try on the group!

Your group of six may decide to commit to each providing two meals per member once every three weeks. A group of four may provide four meals per member every four weeks. The trick is to find the pattern that will best serve the members of your group. You can certainly adjust as you go along, as you strive to find the best rhythm for you.

Q How does your "predetermined budgetary figure" work? I'm looking for hassle-free accounting!

A Our budgetary figure is a number we keep in mind as we select recipes to prepare. Everyone commits to providing the minimum number of entrées agreed upon for this figure, yet has an obligation to provide additional portions when expenses fall below this number. We know that anytime we go over budget it is our gift to the group.

Alternatively, you can keep receipts and adjust for varying costs among group members, or sell your entrées to one another. However, we wouldn't consider this to be a form of hassle-free accounting!

Q I love the idea of providing each group member two, or maybe even three, identical entrées each month. Do you have any recommendations for increasing the variety, without compromising the efficiency?

A You might want to consider getting into a split rotation with your entrées. After your first exchange, put half of the entrées in one place in your freezer, and half in another. Eat only half of your entrées before the next exchange. With your next batch of entrées, place half with last month's remainder, and save half to mix in with half of next month's. And so on.

As your group becomes increasingly savvy, you might begin to incorporate more variety into your menus. Someone making lasagna could easily prepare one beef lasagna and one sausage lasagna. Someone preparing turkey could, with a little extra effort, provide one turkey with wild rice and one roasted turkey with gravy. Someone else may offer to prepare two entirely different recipes.

We do find that we appreciate having two identical entrées on hand for entertaining. We also find that we're often very glad there's a second entrée in the freezer to look forward to because the first one was so delicious! In any case, we believe you will find your family eating a greater variety of foods with *Cooking Among Friends*® than ever before.

Q We don't typically eat "casseroles" or "hot dishes." Do you offer good, freezer-friendly alternatives to the casserole?

A Rest assured. We love good food and abhor mysterious, mushy casseroles. While *Cooking Among Friends*®, the cookbook, offers a number of our favorite comfort foods, we also offer some creative and current alternatives that will thrill your family at dinnertime.

Q What ensures that I'll be trading for meals my family will enjoy . . . and that others in the group will enjoy what I prepare?

A We recommend you establish food preference and preparation guidelines for your group. This will lay the foundation for the types of dishes you will prepare for exchange. We've included an extensive step-by-step checklist to help you establish your group's unique preferences. See *Establishing Group Guidelines.*

Further, the menu for each exchange should be established as a group. Allow each member to give input to recipe selections. We recommend you always pass around a new recipe for perusal. Beef Stroganoff, for example, comes in many different forms. Sharing the recipe will clue everyone in to the end product. The menu should be tweaked until everyone is pleased with the items that will be exchanged.

Q I've noticed your recipes usually do not include convenience items like prepared spaghetti sauces, barbeque sauces, and canned soups. Is this a cost-saving strategy?

A We do recognize the value of prepared items, particularly where the trade-off between cost and time savings is determined to be worthwhile. We also feel that you will be able to prepare a superior product (both in nutrition and flavor), for less cost, by cooking from scratch. This is particularly true when cooking in bulk. However, feel free to substitute prepared sauces as your schedule dictates, budget allows, or as your group prefers!

Q Do you have any recommendations for a group committed to cooking with low-sodium, low-fat ingredients?

A We sometimes substitute "low fat" or "no fat" ingredients in the recipes we prepare. Low sodium, or no sodium, stocks and bouillon can be used. Salt can be eliminated from the recipe. Ground turkey can be substituted for ground beef. While we have not chosen to designate each of our recipes in this way, savvy, health-conscious cooks can easily make the substitutions that will please the members of their exchange group.

Q I don't like to cook, nor do I feel I'm a very good cook! But I love the concept. Do you think there's hope for me?

A It sounds like daily meal preparation is drudgery for you. All the more reason to establish an exchange group! You will be delighted to cook in bulk and have the task completed for many days to come. And we suspect that, even though you don't like to cook, you do have a specialty or two. Volunteer to prepare them for the group, and then work together from there. As your group considers recipes and decides who will prepare which items, choose something you feel comfortable preparing. And enjoy having some of the meal preparation in your home performed by friends!

Q I love to cook. I'm wondering if I'll miss fixing dinner every day!

A We really enjoy cooking, too. *Cooking Among Friends*® gives us more flexibility in deciding when we want to do so! With entrées in the freezer, we've had time to make breads or biscuits, try a new vegetable or salad recipe, or whip up dessert. We still enjoy finding and trying new entrée recipes to prepare for the group. And, as our group prefers not having something in the freezer for every day of the month, we still prepare an entrée every now and then!

We also love to entertain. And *Cooking Among Friends*® has revolutionized hospitality in our homes. The company entrée is often already prepared and in the freezer, thanks to our group of friends. We have learned to be much more effective in personally cooking in bulk (not for exchange) and utilizing our freezers. Mary often has homemade pie shells and frosted brownies in her freezer. They might have been prepared when she tripled up on a pie she prepared for the family and doubled up on brownies needed for a friend's party. You might prepare bread dough today and freeze it for oven-fresh dinner rolls for a dinner party a week from now . . . and oven-fresh cinnamon rolls for breakfast two weeks from now. As you grow more comfortable with freezing food, you'll strategically use your freezer to prepare for anticipated, and unanticipated, entertaining. *Cooking Among Friends*® makes this come naturally!

Q I have several family-favorite recipes. How do I adapt them for *Cooking Among Friends*®?

A Successfully using a favorite recipe requires determining that it freezes well and getting a grip on how much of it to prepare. We have found that four cups of an add-a-side entrée will provide four moderate servings. An add-a-side entrée is a meaty or hearty item that is intended to be served with or over an additional side. Examples include Beef Stroganoff (to be served over noodles or mashed potatoes), Chicken Parmigiana (to be served with side items of your choosing), and Hunan Chicken (to be served over rice). Six cups of a stand-alone entrée will provide four moderate servings. A stand-alone entrée is an item inclusive of rice, pasta, or significant amounts of sauce or vegetables (stews and soups). While you may wish to add side items when serving this item, it is not necessary for the completion of the dish. Examples include Lasagna, White Chicken Chili, and Turkey Pot Pie. We have included *Quantity Equivalents* (see *Resources*) as a guide to help you add up ingredients to arrive at a total volume for any given recipe. When in doubt, prepare more. You'll be far happier to have a couple of extra meals in your freezer than to have come up short.

Q We've formed a group and want to maximize the number of meals we prepare for each exchange. Any suggestions?

A We suggest you determine ways to keep it as simple as possible! In addition to an entrée recipe, consider preparing fill-in items that are quick and easy. You might pop frozen chicken breasts in a freezer bag with a marinade. Consider supplemental meat items that are a spin-off of the main entrée. For example, someone preparing lasagna might also prepare and freeze portions of browned ground beef. (See also *More Mileage from a Single Entrée* in *Going Beyond Entrées*.).

Q I'm forever placing items in my freezer, only to find them months later . . . in a very unappetizing condition! How do you manage your frozen stash?

A You might want to prepare a list of items you take home from each exchange, and then check them off as they are used. This is a wonderful technique for knowing what you have in the freezer. See our form *Keeping It All Together*.

The rhythm of *Cooking Among Friends®* makes it very easy to manage what you have in your freezer. Optimally, your group will work together to establish a food quantity and exchange frequency that allows each member to use up (or nearly use up) one batch of entrées before receiving the next. With this short-term approach to what we place in the freezer, we are all doing a much better job of food management.

Q My freezer space is limited to my refrigerator freezer. Can this technique still work for me?

A Yes! Several of our members are in this situation. While an additional upright or chest freezer is ideal, you can use this program with the freezer space you have. There won't be much room for additional goodies at the beginning of the month (or that liver that has been in there for eight months!), but it can be done.

Q What type of packaging do you use?

A A variety of freezer-friendly packaging is readily available at local grocery stores, discount stores, and wholesale clubs. Our group uses an assortment of aluminum tins with board lids, freezer bags, aluminum foil, and plastic wrap. We have found that our favorite packaging is the aluminum tin with board lid. It is extremely easy to fill and seal, very efficient in space utilization, cost efficient, and aesthetically pleasing! This product, and others, can be ordered directly from *Cooking Among Friends, LLC.* Contact us at our mailing address, e-mail address, website, or by phone.

Q How do I know what will freeze well and what won't?

A The freezing process does change food. The trick to a successful experience with *Cooking Among Friends®* is choosing recipes that freeze well—those that are minimally affected by the freezing process. We have found that it pays to experiment! While cooking references often forbid the freezing of sour cream, we have found that in many recipes where it is whisked into a sauce, it freezes beautifully. Or, at worst, some diligent stirring is required during the reheating process. So don't be afraid to try a family-favorite recipe containing a questionable ingredient by freezing a portion, defrosting, and reheating it for a quality test.

That being said, we do recommend you avoid freezing mayonnaise or sour cream (unless whisked into a sauce), eggs in the shell, lettuce and other greens, cucumbers, radishes, and raw celery.

Q Will I need any special equipment?

A While labor saving kitchen items certainly come in handy, we have not found it absolutely necessary to buy extra equipment. We have been using our electric knives and food processors (it's finally worth getting them dirty!). Extra large containers and pans have been a real asset. And large electrical roasters did end up on everyone's Christmas list within a year of becoming a *Cooking Among Friends®* devotee. They are helpful but not necessary.

Q This technique sounds like a life-saver! How do I get a group started?

A We have some recommendations for you. See *Forming Your Cooking Club.*

Chapter 2

Making It Happen

Forming Your Cooking Club

Perhaps the greatest challenge in establishing a cooking club is finding members! But they're out there, everywhere! Granted, you'll want to have had a peek at their kitchen and have some idea of the types of food they like to prepare. But don't hesitate to ask. Your proposition may very well bring a wonderful blessing to a friend.

Gather your thoughts.

How many meals do you wish to prepare and provide, and how frequently? How many group members would be your ideal? Our group has successfully operated with six members, each member providing two or three identical meals for every member of the group (twelve to eighteen meals). We have also successfully operated as a four-member group, each member providing three or four meals for every member of the group (twelve to sixteen meals). Doing so on a monthly basis has been adequate for us, leaving time for eating out and actually preparing a meal every now and then!

Consider the possibilities.

Potential group members are in your church, workplace, and neighborhood. Friends and family members are wonderful possibilities. Consider the moms and dads from school or day care. And don't forget that group of people you see occasionally due to a common interest (committee, club, prayer or Bible study group, exercise class, league, or diet group). Consider the power of networking. If you, personally, can find a couple of good food exchange members, they in turn might know of a couple more!

Look for similarities.

Your group will be most successful if there is a degree of similarity in family size, family food budget, and food tastes. While family food budget and tastes are significant considerations, a range in family size can be tolerated. Our group is composed of couples and families, our largest family being five members (with young children). You may have a friend with a large family who would like to join a group representing small families. He or she may willingly determine that even though the entrées will be consumed more quickly (i.e. two at a time), it is still a very worthwhile endeavor.

Ask!

Cooking Among Friends, LLC makes it easy to invite friends into a cooking club. Our printed invitations include a spot for you to address and sign the card, as well as a place to indicate your method of follow-up. Six invitations are included in our organizational kit, *Getting Started & Keeping It All Together.* (Invitations are also available in packages of six directly from *Cooking Among Friends, LLC.* Contact us at our mailing address, e-mail address, website, or by phone.)

You might wish to invite interested members to an informational meeting where you elaborate further on the *Cooking Among Friends*® concept and discuss the possibilities. Or, better yet, if your invitations immediately inspire a committed group of friends, get together to establish your group's guidelines, decide upon your first menu, and set the date for your first exchange!

Establish your group's unique guidelines.

Will you prepare mild or spicy foods? Do members prefer white meat or dark meat, whole grains or processed grains? Does anyone have an allergy or diet restriction? What size entrée will sufficiently feed the families represented in the group, and become the standard?

Obviously there are a number of issues. And the more issues you address up-front, in advance, the more successful your group will be. *Cooking Among Friends*® provides an aid for establishing your group's unique preferences. Our form entitled *Establishing Group Guidelines* (see *Resources*) may be photocopied and circulated among potential group members. Request that each person complete the form, indicating his or her unique food preferences. Then work together to arrive at consensus as a group. We recommend you then complete your *Official Group Guidelines* (see *Resources*). Copy and circulate this form back to group members. This form will serve as a valuable resource should any questions arise, and a valuable aid should you need to add a new member to your group.

Start simple . . . get started!

Cooking Among Friends® presents a lot of information. So many strategies, so many possibilities. Recognizing that you may be overwhelmed by choice and opportunity, we recommend you simply get started! You may only have three friends committed to *Cooking Among Friends*®. Start there! You may decide to add more members later, or decide it's working great with the four of you! Maybe you think you'd like to exchange breakfast items in addition to your entrées. . . but cookie dough sounds good, too. May we recommend that you start exchanging entrées, and experiment from there? Let your group be a work in process, fine-tuning and tweaking until it's just right for you.

Preparing Your Entrée

We'd all say we've come a long way since we first attacked twenty-five pounds of meat, armed with a kitchen knife, and turned it into twelve fabulous meals. We've learned a couple of tricks along the way, and preparing meals for exchange has become much easier than it used to be! If you find that cooking in these quantities is intimidating, don't despair. You, too, will learn effective strategies. Within no time at all, you'll consider yourself a pro. We'll even venture to guess you'll never cook in single-meal quantities again.

Minimize the stress and workload of preparing your meals by giving careful consideration to the recipe you choose, and by taking some simple preparatory measures in the weeks and days ahead. Remember that even the simplest of advanced preparations can make you feel well ahead of the game.

Consider the Recipe

Count the cost of preparing intricate recipes and save them for when you have the extra time and energy to go the extra mile. Or, consider preparing entrées with a friend. You might strategize to work together to prepare one labor-intensive recipe and one simple recipe. You'll enjoy one another's company and appreciate sharing the workload of the challenging recipe.

Weeks Ahead

- Watch grocery store fliers for sale ingredients.
- Inform group members of exceptional sales.
- Block out your cooking time on the calendar. Avoid scheduling too close to the exchange date.

Days Ahead

- Check supply of all recipe ingredients.
- Check supply of all packaging materials.
- Make any last minute shopping trips.
- Prepare labels.
- Prepare reheating instructions.
- Label all packaging materials.
- Strategize the most efficient way to prepare your recipe (i.e. in batches, in multiple cooking periods).
- Place large meat items in the refrigerator to defrost according to proper guidelines.

The Day Before

- Lower your freezer temperature, if desired.
- Clear storage space in your freezer.
- Clear shelves in your refrigerator.
- Prepare any elements of the recipe that will make your cooking session easier.
    - Cut up vegetables.
    - Cook and debone meat.
    - Premeasure or portion ingredients.
    - Carefully refrigerate perishable items in airtight containers.

The Big Event

- Dress comfortably.
- Consider wearing an apron to protect your clothing.
- Work during the time of day you're most efficient.
- Distract the kids.
- Clear kitchen counters of unnecessary items.
- Set out necessary appliances and utensils so they are easily accessible.
- Place a trashcan within easy reach.
- Place hand towels within easy reach.
- Clean up as you go.
- Pour a cup of your favorite beverage . . . play some enjoyable music! The time expended is well worth your effort.

The Exchange

For your *Cooking Among Friends*® group to be most successful, we recommend you establish a group facilitator. This person will handle the administrative aspects of maintaining your group, communicate any necessary notices or reminders, and facilitate the "business" portion of the exchange gathering.

What effective system isn't complete without a little (ugh!) paperwork? While your group may take a very casual approach, we have found it helpful to get some things down on paper (or bits and bytes). Our forms have been developed for this purpose (see *Resources*).

Exchange entrées!

Bring your entrées to the exchange gathering in coolers. Provide a large, cleared area where everyone can unpack their frozen goods and then take turns distributing them. Repack the coolers. The items will easily remain frozen while you discuss necessary business and enjoy your time together.

Take care of business.

- For effective food management, allow time for everyone to compile a list of items that will be taken home and placed in the freezer. It is helpful to also note extra ingredients that will be stored in the pantry. We have found it easy to overlook these items when we reheat a meal. See our form *Keeping It All Together*.

- Evaluate the previous menu and determine which entrées are eligible for repetition. Add them to your list of favorite food exchange recipes. See our form *Favorite Exchange Recipes*.

  Alternatively, you may wish to provide an evaluation form so everyone can give open feedback without concern for hurting another's feelings. See our form *Keeping It All Together*. Your group facilitator may wish to collect this form from each group member, compile responses away from the group, and add favorites to the list of favorite exchange recipes. An updated list would then be circulated to group members. Non-favorites would fall discreetly from memory.

- Plan and record the upcoming menu, deciding who will prepare each item. See our form *Keeping It All Together*.

- Solicit any requests for the exchange of additional food items. Allow menu selections and quantities to be determined by those who elect to participate.

- Determine the recipient of your *Culinary TLC* meals, if applicable, and who will deliver them. Consider including a card signed by each member of the group.

- Set the date, time, and place of your next exchange gathering.

Have a wonderful time!

Your group may have elected a "business only" approach to food exchange. Or you may have elected to take this opportunity to enjoy one another's company. If so, have a wonderful time! Celebrate a re-stocked freezer! We have found our exchange gatherings to be a welcomed chance to catch up with each other and have fun. We hope *Cooking Among Friends*® brings a refreshing and strengthening rhythm of friendship into your life.

Chapter 3

Going Beyond Entrées

Going Beyond Entrées

Cooking Among Friends® is loaded with opportunity! While each member of our group has committed to prepare entrées for exchange on a regular basis, we have an open invitation to propose additional items at any time. If, for example, one of us would like to have an assortment of party foods in the freezer, we would ask if any other members would like to participate in an appetizer exchange. All have the option of opting in or out of this supplemental exchange. Quantities and recipes are worked out among those who elect to participate. Consider these possibilities.

Cookie Dough

One of our favorite swaps is frozen cookie dough! Having a varied supply on hand means we're well prepared for last minute entertaining, after school snacks, or late night cravings for chocolate chip cookies fresh from the oven. Making a jumbo batch is easy! Just divide, freeze, swap and enjoy.

Baked Goods

Baked goods freeze beautifully and are a pleasure to serve to family and friends. Consider exchanging muffins, quick breads, pastries, yeast breads, or rolls. Items that can be frozen before baking, such as yeast breads and pastries, are particularly enjoyable because they can later be served fresh from the oven.

Desserts

Our group has fallen into a pattern of being regular dessert exchangers! The brownies, cheesecakes, ice cream cakes, bars, apple crisps, frosted cakes, and pies that have lingered for but a short while on our freezer shelves have been truly delectable. Having them in the freezer makes it so much easier to add an occasional festive note to an evening meal, entertain friends, or celebrate an occasion.

Soup's On!

Perhaps you'll want to commit an exchange to filling your freezer with delectable soups. Whether you prepare soups as a supplement to your entrée exchange, or simply plan to do a few soups among your other entrées, many freeze beautifully and are particularly pleasing to have in the freezer during the fall and winter months. You might consider freezing soup in individual portions. The portions will be ready to grab for lunches, or for evenings when household members are on the go and a more elaborate meal just isn't necessary . . . or convenient!

The Holiday Meal

Hosting the holiday meal is always a little stressful. Prepare ahead and do your cooking among friends. At the exchange prior to the holiday meal, each member could provide a single frozen item for every member participating. Your established Thanksgiving menu might include stuffing, a sweet potato bake, a vegetable casserole, twice-baked potatoes, yeast rolls, pies (frozen before baking), and frozen punch. Supplement with a roasted turkey on Thanksgiving Day, and any other necessities, and your holiday meal is complete!

The Farmer's Market

Your food exchange group might pull together to freeze some of the produce available in season at local farmer's markets and orchards (or your own garden plot). Decide which items all participants would like to freeze for the winter months. Establish who among the group will purchase, prepare, and freeze which item(s). It is our recommendation that you determine a budgetary figure and allow it to dictate quantity (all will spend the same amount to purchase what will be varying quantities of specific items). Your group might enjoy freezing peaches, strawberries, blueberries, fresh corn, and green beans. Get together in pairs to prepare and freeze items that are labor intensive.

Party Foods

Is there anything more time challenging than preparing a variety of beautiful hors d'oeuvres for an event? This, too, is something that you can divide and conquer among your *Cooking Among Friends®* group. Consider this supplemental exchange for the holiday season, or just to have appetizers in the freezer for last minute entertaining! Establish a menu and decide who will prepare each item. Arrive at the exchange with a large quantity of grilled chicken skewers (with marinade for reheating), and leave with miniature reubens ready for grilling, savory turnovers, stuffed mushrooms, spinach phyllo packets, and a cheese spread. It's a party waiting to happen! May we also suggest a dessert buffet?

Breakfast

By cooking among friends, you can come together and help one another conquer "the most important meal of the day." A trip down the grocery store freezer aisle will offer some great ideas and remind you that you can prepare a far superior frozen breakfast item for a great deal less expense. Your family might enjoy quiches, breakfast pies, biscuits with egg and/or meat, pigs in blankets, waffles, pancakes, french toast, quick breads, muffins, or doughnuts.

Ice Cream & Sorbet

You might even want to exchange homemade ice cream! It's so easy to make a big batch of a single ice cream recipe. Prepare and freeze it in pint or quart-sized containers. Trade your vanilla ice cream for one each of chocolate, banana rum, mocha almond fudge, strawberry, and peach. Your family will be delighted. And if you're hosting a party, you'll have on hand the makings of some spectacular sundaes!

Marinades & Sauces

For summer meal preparation, a varied supply of marinades and dipping sauces goes a long, long way! You might consider taking a month off from your traditional entrée exchange and plan to grill. Supply one another with sauces and recipes or ideas for their use. Everyone can stock up on preferred meats and look forward to a lot of outdoor cooking. (There are, of course, a number of items that can be frozen ahead for future grilling. Consider stuffed burgers, pizzas, beef kabobs with blanched vegetables, and individual foil packet meals. Frozen chicken breasts can be placed in a freezer bag containing marinade, and popped back into the freezer before defrosting for future grilling.)

More Mileage from a Single Entrée

Your *Cooking Among Friends*® group can supplement entrée exchanges with items that are almost an entrée! Having browned ground beef in the freezer puts you one significant step closer to whipping up spaghetti or tacos. If an exchange member is already preparing lasagna for exchange, why not brown extra ground beef, bag it, and freeze? Frozen poached chicken breasts quickly become chicken salad or pasta toppers. Frozen roasted turkey meat quickly becomes a delicious sandwich or soup. Frozen cooked beef can be transformed into beef barbecue or stew. Even raw chicken breasts, frozen with a marinade, will have you ready to grill, or to slice up for fajitas! With a little extra effort, you can capitalize on the entrée being prepared by planning extra meat for exchange. With cooked meats in the freezer, in addition to your entrées, you will be even more prepared for meals to come.

Culinary TLC

One of the truly great benefits of preparing and freezing meals in advance is not only having a supply in the freezer for your own family, but also for the occasional need that arises in the lives of friends and other family members. You'll find yourself prepared to respond with a little culinary TLC when a friend has a baby, you hear of a neighbor experiencing a loss, or a co-worker is battling an illness. Your group may wish to become intentional about sharing frozen entrées. Our group has done this on a regular basis by each member preparing one extra frozen meal per exchange. Our TLC meals are placed together and delivered to a recipient (or recipients) in need.

Holiday Gifts from the Pantry

Your group may wish to work together to do homemade holiday gift giving! Simply exchanging cookies, bars, or candy for each member to package greatly simplifies the preparation of lovely holiday gifts. You may wish to plan the look and theme of your final gift as a group and allow each member to contribute toward its completion. Give a gift of breakfast in bed! Include a pancake or scone mix, granola, syrup or jam, jarred fruit compote, ground nut butter, and a flavored coffee, tea, or cocoa mix. Someone's contribution might be designing and making the packaging (or doing the legwork to purchase!). Give a gift of holiday cookie decorating

Assemble kits including shaped cookies, bagged frostings in various colors, and assorted sprinkles. The possibilities are endless! Just remember to work out an agreeable and equitable financial arrangement in advance.

Staples Stock-Up

Consider adding a quarterly, semi-annual, or annual stock-up to your regularly scheduled entrée exchange gatherings. Adopting a food co-operative strategy, your group can purchase staples in bulk from a restaurant supply store or bulk warehouse and divide them among group members. Not only will you realize significant financial savings, but you may also find you are able to reduce your grocery store shopping list to fresh foods (dairy, fruits, vegetables) and few other items. Your staples stock-up list might include flour, cornmeal, oatmeal, sugars, spices, pastas, noodles, and rice. We recommend you establish a commitment among the group to divide 100% of each item purchased and allow group members to purchase varying quantities of each item. This might also be an effective strategy for stocking your freezer with preferred frozen fruits, vegetables, breads, and juices.

Dry Mixes

Dry mixes are becoming increasingly popular and intriguing recipes abound! Preparing them in bulk radically slashes prices found in grocery store gourmet aisles and at in-home parties. Consider preparing in bulk the mixes your group members would like to have in the cupboard. Suggestions include dip and dressing mixes, cookie and bar mixes, spice rubs, marinades, curries, beer bread mixes, cake mixes, and drink mixes. With some creative packaging, these items can also become wonderful gifts and would be ideal for housewarmings, showers, teacher appreciation, welcoming a new neighbor, or thanking a hostess!

The Mini-Exchange

Our group regularly has members wheeling and dealing on the side. If your family could use additional entrées, or if you find yourself craving a supply of an entrée not included on the upcoming menu, propose a supplemental mini-exchange with another member of the group. Offer to prepare lasagnas in exchange for a friend's turkey pot pies. It's a great way to add extra items to your freezer!

Kid Pleasers

If your group represents a hungry crowd of youngsters, preparing and freezing kid pleasers may be just the ticket to easy, nutritious lunches or a compromise when finicky eaters balk at the evening menu. Prepare, freeze, and exchange wraps, chicken tenders, a less dreadful macaroni and cheese, meatballs, and mini-burgers. You may wish to prepare items for school lunches. Choose recipes that will travel easily and package them individually so they're ready to pop into a sack or lunchbox. Frozen items will defrost by lunchtime. And having lunch's "main dish" prepared ahead will make your morning a little less harried!

Á la Carte

Your group members may wish to exchange side items along with entrées, finding yourselves devoted to having rice pilaf, scalloped potatoes, stuffing, cauliflower au gratin, or broccoli with a cheese sauce in your freezer. While our group has not incorporated a group-wide side exchange into our menus, we do occasionally include an accompaniment with a main dish. Receiving stuffing with Roasted Turkey and Cranberries, scalloped potatoes with Country Meatloaf, or rice pilaf with Moroccan Beef is a welcomed and appreciated bonus.

There are so many ways that you can pull together as a group and support one another with food preparation! We believe that your *Cooking Among Friends*® group will discover its unique preferences and fall into its own rhythm. You may be among avid cookie lovers, and prepare cookie dough every month! You may be among parents of school age children, and appreciate having nutritional breakfast items prepared ahead. Let ideas flow, experiment, and you will discover what works best for, and is most pleasing to, the members of your group!

Chapter 4

Entrée Recipes

Entrée Recipes

Both on our website and in our cookbook we've assembled an eclectic mix of our favorite recipes. As the variety implies, and you will discover, *Cooking Among Friends®* can be as comforting as Meatloaf and Turkey Pot Pie, as kid-friendly as Pizza Burgers and Sloppy Joes, or as globe trotting as Moroccan Beef and Hunan Chicken. Our group has enjoyed mixing traditional favorites with current and more exotic fare. We thought yours would, too.

Cooking Among Friends® can mean great food. If you're feeling squeamish about coming home to a frozen entrée, let us reassure you. Your dining experience can be as good as a meal in the restaurant of your favorite celebrity chef, or Sunday dinner at Grandma's house. All it takes is a good, freezer-friendly recipe and quality ingredients.

Practicalities

Most recipes are indicated in six-meal, twelve-meal, and eighteen-meal quantities (with each meal providing four moderate servings). You will find that you prepare some recipes in batches. You may need to prepare eighteen meals, for example, and do so by simmering three different pots containing six meals each. You'll find it easier to work from the six-meal ingredients list to appropriately portion ingredients. If, however, you have a large electrical roaster, you'll be able to work directly from the eighteen-meal ingredients list and simmer everything together in a single batch.

Strategies

We'd all say we've come a long way since we first attacked twenty-five pounds of meat, armed with a kitchen knife, and turned it into twelve fabulous meals. We've learned a couple of tricks along the way, and preparing our meals for exchange has become much easier than it used to be! So if you find that cooking in these quantities is intimidating, don't despair. You, too, will learn effective strategies. Within no time at all, you'll consider yourself a pro. We'll even venture to guess you'll never cook in single-meal quantities again.

De-intensify your cooking period (both in terms of time and energy) by spreading it over multiple time frames. For each recipe, *Divide and Conquer* lists steps you can perform the day before, or days before, your final cooking period. Pick the things you can most conveniently, and/or strategically, do ahead. Tips are included to pass along little tidbits we've picked up along the way, or to perhaps inspire a unique solution of your own for a challenge you've encountered. We hope you find them helpful.

Preparing *Your* Favorite Recipes

Successfully using a favorite recipe requires determining that it freezes well and getting a grip on how much of it to prepare. We have found that one cup of an add-a-side entrée will provide one moderate serving. An add-a-side entrée is a meaty or hearty item intended to be served with or over an additional side. Examples include Beef Stroganoff (to be served over noodles or mashed potatoes), Chicken Parmigiana (to be served with side items of your choosing), and Hunan Chicken (to be served over rice). One and a half cups of a stand-alone entrée will provide one moderate serving. A stand-alone entrée is an item inclusive of rice, pasta, or significant amounts of sauce or vegetables (stews and soups). While you may wish to add side items when serving this item, it is not necessary for the completion of the dish. Examples include Lasagna, White Chicken Chili, and Turkey Pot Pie. We have included *Quantity Equivalents* (see *Resources*) as a guide to help you add up ingredients to arrive at a total volume for any given recipe. When in doubt, prepare more. You'll be far happier to have a couple of extra meals in your freezer than to have come up short.

Simmering on the Stovetop and in the Oven

Your collection of pots, pans, Dutch ovens, and roasters might indicate your best strategy is to simmer on the stovetop and in the oven. Where recipes indicate simmering on the stovetop, feel free to simmer in the oven at 350°, and vice versa.

The Mysteries of Reducing

Some of our recipes include instructions for reducing sauces or stocks. This process of simmering a pot, uncovered, allows liquid to evaporate and results in a thicker, more intensely flavored product. We have attempted to provide a time guideline for reducing sauces. However, the size of your batches (as indicated by the sizes of your available pots and pans) will influence the duration of simmering. Generally, the smaller the batch, the more quickly it will reduce. If you find you've over-reduced, add liquid, cup by cup, until you're satisfied with the consistency. You may wish to purchase extra cream, wine, tomato sauce, or broth (as appropriate to the recipe) for this purpose.

Beef Recipes

Preparing Beef
Beef Paprika
Beef Burgundy
Beef Fajita Kits
Beef Pot Pie with Cheddar Cheese Crust
Beef Stroganoff
Indonesian Beef
Citrus Glazed Corned Beef
Irish Beef Stew
Italian Swiss Steak
Moroccan Beef
Roast Barbecue
Orange Beef
Roast Beef with Carrots
Rueben Loaf Kits
South African Beef Stew

(See also Going Beyond Entrée Recipes – Soup's On)

Preparing Beef

Braising and Stewing Beef

Beef roast
Water
Salt and pepper

For each 10 pounds of beef:

3 large celery ribs, cut into 2-inch pieces
1 large onion, quartered
1 large carrot, cut into 2-inch pieces

In a large skillet or Dutch oven over medium-high heat, heat oil. Season roast with salt and pepper and brown on all sides. Transfer meat from browning pan to roasting pan. Place vegetables alongside roast. Season vegetables with salt and pepper. Add enough water so roast is half covered. Simmer meat on stovetop or in a 325° oven 3 to 4 hours or until roast is fork tender, turning roast occasionally. Remove meat from pan. Reserve juices for use in recipe if desired.

Boiling Corned Beef

Fresh corned beef
Water

For each 10 pounds of corned beef:

2 medium onions
8 whole cloves
1 tablespoon garlic
2 large carrots, cut into 2-inch pieces
2 large celery ribs, cut into 2-inch pieces
Ground black pepper

Place corned beef in a large stockpot or roaster and add enough water to cover. Peel onions and stud each one with 4 whole cloves. Add to beef, along with garlic, carrots, and celery. Season with pepper. Bring to boil over medium-high heat. Reduce heat to low, cover, and simmer until beef is tender (approximately 3½ hours). Alternatively, roast, covered, in 325° oven until tender. Turn beef over every hour while cooking.

Beef Paprika

Makes 6, 12, or 18 4-serving meals

(approximately 1 cup per serving)

Recommended Packaging

aluminum tins with board lids

plastic wrap

Ingredients and Instructions

meals	12 meals	18 meals	
4 servings	48 servings	72 servings	
			olive or vegetable oil
0 pounds	20 pounds	30 pounds	beef cut into 1-inch chunks
			salt and pepper

Work in batches as necessary. In a large skillet or Dutch oven over medium-high heat, heat oil. Season and brown beef chunks. Refrigerate. Reserve meat juices and reduce to taste.

			olive or vegetable oil
	12	18	medium onions, chopped
½ cups	3 cups	4½ cups	sweet paprika (Hungarian is preferred, but Spanish may be substituted)
tablespoon	2 tablespoons	3 tablespoons	salt
cups	8 cups	12 cups	beef stock or canned broth (include reserved meat juices)
8 ounces	56 ounces	84 ounces	canned chopped or stewed tomatoes, undrained
2 ounces	24 ounces	36 ounces	tomato paste
pounds	6 pounds	9 pounds	sour cream

Work in batches as necessary. In a large stockpot over medium heat, heat oil. Sauté onions until tender. Add paprika and salt, cooking and stirring minutes. Stir in beef stock or canned broth, tomatoes, and tomato paste and bring to a boil at high heat. Add browned beef chunks. Reduce eat, cover, and simmer until meat is tender (approximately 2 to 2 ½ hours). Remove from heat. Stir in sour cream. Divide evenly among tins. ool. Cover with a sheet of plastic wrap, pressing down to cling to food. Apply board lid. Freeze.

Reheating Instructions

Defrost in refrigerator. Remove board lid and plastic wrap. Transfer to saucepan or microwave safe dish and heat thoroughly. Serve over oodles or mashed potatoes.

Divide and Conquer

- Strategize batch sizes based on available containers/cookware.
- Cube beef.
- Brown beef.
- Chop and sauté onions.
- Prepare and label all packaging.

Portion entrées more evenly by straining broth or sauce from other ingredients. Divide strained ingredients between containers and top with sauce.

Beef Burgundy

Makes 6, 12, or 18 4-serving meals

(approximately 1 cup per serving)

Divide and Conquer

- Strategize batch sizes based on available containers/cookware.
- Cook and chop bacon.
- Cube beef.
- Brown beef.
- Chop and sauté vegetables.
- Clean and slice mushrooms.
- Prepare and label all packaging.

Recommended Packaging

aluminum tins with board lids
plastic wrap

Ingredients and Instructions

6 meals 24 servings	12 meals 48 servings	18 meals 72 servings	
			olive or vegetable oil
9 pounds	18 pounds	27 pounds	beef cut into 1-inch chunks
			salt and pepper

Work in batches as necessary. In a large skillet or Dutch oven over medium-high heat, heat oil. Season and brown beef chunks. Refrigerate. Reserve meat juices and reduce to taste.

1½ pounds	3 pounds	4½ pounds	bacon

Work in batches as necessary. In the same skillet over medium heat (or in oven), cook bacon until crisp. Drain and crumble or chop bacon. Refrigerate.

			olive oil or bacon fat
6	12	18	medium onions, chopped
2 pounds	4 pounds	6 pounds	carrots, sliced
5 cups	10 cups	15 cups	dry red wine (Burgundy or Cabernet)
7 cups	14 cups	21 cups	beef stock or canned broth (include reserved meat juices)
40 ounces	80 ounces	7 lbs, 8 oz	canned diced tomatoes, undrained
1 tablespoon	2 tablespoons	3 tablespoons	sugar
8	16	24	bay leaves
2 tablespoons	¼ cup	6 tablespoons	dried thyme
2 pounds	4 pounds	6 pounds	fresh mushrooms, halved (optional)
			salt and pepper to taste

Work in batches as necessary. In a large stockpot over medium heat, heat oil. Sauté onions and carrots until tender. Stir in wine, beef stock or canned broth, tomatoes, sugar, bay leaves, and thyme and bring to a boil at high heat. Add browned beef chunks and chopped bacon. Reduce heat, cover, and simmer until meat is tender (approximately 2 to 2½ hours). When meat is tender, stir in mushrooms and cook 15 minutes. Remove and discard bay leaves. Remove any fat from the surface of the liquid. Season with salt and pepper.

| 1 cup | 2 cups | 3 cups | cold water |
| ½ cup | 1 cup | 1½ cups | all-purpose flour |

In a separate dish, stir flour and water until blended (use a blender if necessary). Slowly stir flour and water into beef mixture. Continue simmering over low heat, uncovered, until mixture slightly thickens. Divide evenly among tins. Cool. Cover with a sheet of plastic wrap, pressing down to cling to food. Apply board lid. Freeze.

Reheating Instructions

Defrost in refrigerator. Remove board lid and plastic wrap. Transfer to saucepan or microwave safe dish and heat thoroughly. Serve over rice, noodles, or mashed potatoes.

Lower the cost of preparing a recipe by adjusting it to include more sauce and less meat.

Beef Fajita Kits

Makes 6, 12, or 18 4-serving meals

(2 fajitas per serving)

| Recommended Packaging | | | one gallon freezer bags
one quart freezer bags
sandwich bags
plastic wrap |

Ingredients and Instructions

6 meals 24 servings	12 meals 48 servings	18 meals 72 servings	
9 pounds	**18 pounds**	**27 pounds**	skirt or flank steak, visible fat trimmed
1½ cups	**3 cups**	**4½ cups**	fresh lime juice
¾ cup	**1½ cups**	**2¼ cups**	olive oil
¼ cup	**½ cup**	**¾ cup**	garlic, minced or pressed
3 tablespoons	**6 tablespoons**	**9 tablespoons**	ground cumin
2 tablespoons	**¼ cup**	**6 tablespoons**	salt

In a medium bowl, whisk together lime juice, olive oil, garlic, cumin, and salt. Cover steak with marinade, turning to coat. Marinate, refrigerated, 24 hours. Remove steak from marinade, discarding marinade. Grill steak on hot grill. Alternatively, broil approximately 4 inches under a preheated broiler. Test for doneness after 5 minutes on each side. Allow steak to thoroughly cool. Slice very thinly, perpendicular to the grain. Refrigerate.

			olive oil
6	12	18	jumbo onions, sliced
1½ teaspoons	1 tablespoon	4½ teaspoons	ground cumin
1½ teaspoons	1 tablespoon	4½ teaspoons	paprika
1½ teaspoons	1 tablespoon	4½ teaspoons	dried thyme
1½ teaspoons	1 tablespoon	4½ teaspoons	dried oregano
1½ teaspoons	1 tablespoon	4½ teaspoons	garlic salt

Work in batches as necessary. In a large skillet over medium-high heat, heat oil. Sauté onions until softened. Increasing heat if necessary, brown some of the onions. Add spices and stir approximately 2 minutes. Remove from heat. Divide steak and onions evenly among one quart freezer bags, shaking to combine. Seal bag, pressing out excess air.

48	96	144	7-inch to 8-inch flour tortillas
12 cups	24 cups	36 cups	cheddar cheese, shredded

Wrap flour tortillas in plastic wrap (8 tortillas per meal or 2 per serving). Package cheese in sandwich bags (2 cups per meal or ½ cup per serving). Place a package of beef, a package of tortillas, and a package of cheese in each one gallon freezer bag. Seal bag, pressing out excess air. Freeze.

Reheating Instructions

Defrost in refrigerator. Preheat oven to 350°. Remove packaging. Transfer beef to a baking dish and reheat approximately 15 minutes. Warm tortillas in oven or microwave. Serve with shredded cheese. Add shredded lettuce, chopped tomatoes, sour cream, and salsa as desired.

Beef Pot Pie with Cheddar Cheese Crust

Makes 6, 12, or 18 4-serving meals

(approximately 1½ cups per serving)

Recommended Packaging

5"x12" or 8"x 8" (6-cup) aluminum tins
with board lids
plastic wrap

Ingredients and Instructions

6 meals 24 servings	12 meals 48 servings	18 meals 72 servings	
15 pounds	**30 pounds**	**45 pounds**	**lean beef roast**

Cook beef. See *Preparing Beef*. Cool. Cut into ½-inch cubes, discarding any fat or gristle. Refrigerate. Reserve stock and reduce to taste.

			olive or vegetable oil
4	**8**	**12**	**medium onions, chopped**
2 pounds	**4 pounds**	**6 pounds**	**carrots, diced**
2 tablespoons	**¼ cup**	**6 tablespoons**	**garlic, pressed or minced**

Work in batches as necessary. In a large skillet or Dutch oven over medium heat, heat oil. Sauté onion, carrots, and garlic until tender. Remove from pan and set aside.

2¼ cups	**4½ cups**	**6¾ cups**	**all-purpose flour**
2¼ cups	**4½ cups**	**6¾ cups**	**butter**
9 cups	**18 cups**	**27 cups**	**beef stock or canned broth (include reserved stock)**
7 cups	**14 cups**	**21 cups**	**chicken stock or canned broth**
6 tablespoons	**¾ cup**	**1 cup plus 2 tablespoons**	**creamed horseradish**
24 ounces	**48 ounces**	**72 ounces**	**frozen corn**
16 ounces	**32 ounces**	**48 ounces**	**frozen peas**
			salt and pepper to taste

Work in batches as necessary. In a large skillet over medium heat, melt butter. Stir in flour and cook 3 to 5 minutes. Slowly add beef and chicken stock or canned broth, stirring constantly until well blended. Whisk over medium heat until thickened. Stir in creamed horseradish. Remove from heat and transfer to a large container for combining ingredients. Stir in reserved beef, corn, and peas until combined. Season with salt and pepper. Divide evenly among tins. Cover with Cheddar Cheese Crust. Cover with a sheet of plastic wrap, pressing down to cling to food. Apply board lid. Freeze.

Cheddar Cheese Crust

6 crusts	12 crusts	18 crusts	
6 cups	12 cups	12 cups	all-purpose flour
1 tablespoon	2 tablespoons	3 tablespoons	salt
2 cups	4 cups	6 cups	shortening
2 cups	4 cups	6 cups	shredded cheddar cheese
1 cup	2 cups	3 cups	ice water

A prepared pie crust is a labor-saving option for pot pies!

Work in batches of no more than 6 crusts. In a large bowl, combine flour and salt. Using a fork or pastry blender, cut shortening into flour and salt mixture until it resembles coarse crumbs. Stir in shredded cheese. Sprinkle with ice water, adding approximately ¼ cup at a time. Continue adding water until dough is just moist enough to form a ball when lightly pressed together. Divide dough into desired number of crusts, wrap in plastic wrap, and refrigerate 30 minutes. After removing from refrigerator, let crusts set at room temperature 10 minutes before rolling. Roll each crust on a floured surface, cutting to fit size of tin (use board lid as template). Stack crusts on a cookie sheet, using a sheet of plastic wrap to divide crusts. Refrigerate.

Using a food processor, work in batches of 2 crusts each (dividing the 6 crust ingredient list). Place flour, salt, and shortening in processor bowl with metal blade. Process until mixture resembles coarse crumbs. Add shredded cheese and incorporate. With machine running, add water through the feed tube. Process until a ball forms. Divide each ball into 2 crusts, wrap in plastic wrap, and refrigerate 30 minutes. After removing from refrigerator, let crusts set at room temperature 10 minutes before rolling. Roll each crust on a floured surface, cutting to fit size of tin (use board lid as template). Stack crusts on a cookie sheet, using a sheet of plastic wrap to divide crusts. Refrigerate.

Reheating Instructions

Defrost in refrigerator. Preheat oven to 375°. Remove board lid and plastic wrap. Cover loosely with foil to prevent drying. Bake until bubbly around edges and hot in center (approximately 40 minutes). Let stand at room temperature 15 minutes before cutting.

Beef Stroganoff

Makes 6, 12, or 18 4-serving meals

(approximately 1 cup per serving)

We have adapted traditional recipes like Beef Stroganoff to use an inexpensive cut of meat that has been roasted at a low heat for a long period. More tender cuts of beef (filet mignon, top sirloin, etc.) may be cut into strips and briefly sautéed before being added to the recipe.

Recommended Packaging

aluminum tins with board lids
plastic wrap

Ingredients and Instructions

6 meals	12 meals	18 meals	
24 servings	48 servings	72 servings	
10 pounds	**20 pounds**	**30 pounds**	**lean beef roast**

Cook beef. See *Preparing Beef*. Cool. Cut into bite-sized pieces, discarding any fat or gristle. Refrigerate. Reserve stock and reduce to taste.

¼ cup	**½ cup**	**¾ cup**	**butter**
5	**10**	**15**	**large onions, finely chopped**
2 pounds	**4 pounds**	**6 pounds**	**fresh mushrooms, sliced**

Work in batches as necessary. In a large skillet or Dutch oven over medium heat, melt butter. Sauté onions and mushrooms until tender. Remove from pan and set aside.

¾ cup	**1½ cups**	**2¼ cups**	**butter**
1 cup	**2 cups**	**3 cups**	**all-purpose flour**
10 cups	**20 cups**	**30 cups**	**beef stock or canned broth (include reserved stock)**
1¼ cups	**2½ cups**	**3¾ cups**	**dry red wine (Burgundy or Cabernet)**
3 tablespoons	**6 tablespoons**	**9 tablespoons**	**Dijon mustard**
2 tablespoons	**¼ cup**	**6 tablespoons**	**dried dill**
1½ pounds	**3 pounds**	**4½ pounds**	**sour cream**
			salt and pepper to taste

Work in batches as necessary. In a large skillet over medium heat, melt butter. Stir in flour and cook 3 to 5 minutes. Slowly add beef stock or canned broth, stirring constantly until well blended. Stir in wine, mustard, and dill. Whisk over medium heat until thickened. Stir in reserved onion and mushroom mixture. Remove from heat and transfer to a large container for combining ingredients. Stir in sour cream. Season with salt and pepper. Gently stir in reserved beef. Divide evenly among tins. Cool. Cover with a sheet of plastic wrap, pressing down to cling to food. Apply board lid. Freeze.

Reheating Instructions

Defrost in refrigerator. Remove board lid and plastic wrap. Transfer to saucepan or microwave safe dish and heat thoroughly. Serve over noodles, mashed potatoes, or buttered toast triangles.

Indonesian Beef

Makes 6, 12, or 18 4-serving meals

(approximately 1 cup per serving)

Recommended Packaging   aluminum tins with board lids
plastic wrap

Ingredients and Instructions

_ meals / 24 servings_	12 meals / 48 servings	18 meals / 72 servings	
			olive or vegetable oil
_ pounds	20 pounds	30 pounds	beef cut into 1-inch chunks
			salt and pepper

Work in batches as necessary. In a large skillet or Dutch oven over medium-high heat, heat oil. Season and brown beef chunks. Refrigerate. Discard meat juices.

			olive or vegetable oil
	4	6	medium onions, chopped
_ tablespoons	¾ cup	1 cup plus 2 tablespoons	fresh ginger, minced
_ teaspoons	8 teaspoons	¼ cup	garlic, pressed or minced
	8	12	jalapeno peppers, seeded and diced
_ teaspoon	2 teaspoons	1 tablespoon	ground cumin
_ teaspoon	2 teaspoons	1 tablespoon	cayenne pepper
_ cup	1½ cups	2¼ cups	brown sugar, packed
_ cup	1 cup	1½ cups	soy sauce
_ cup	1 cup	1½ cups	fresh lime juice
_ ounces	7 lbs, 5 oz	11 lbs, 4 oz	canned diced tomatoes, slightly drained
	4	6	green bell peppers, seeded and sliced
_ pounds	4 pounds	6 pounds	fresh mushrooms, sliced (optional)

Work in batches as necessary. In a stockpot over medium heat, heat oil. Sauté onions, ginger, garlic, jalapeno peppers, cumin, and cayenne pepper until onions are tender. Stir in brown sugar, soy sauce, lime juice, tomatoes, and bell peppers. Add browned beef chunks. Reduce heat, cover, and simmer until meat is tender (approximately 2 to 2½ hours). Stir in sliced mushrooms and cook uncovered 10 minutes. Divide evenly among tins. Cool. Cover with a sheet of plastic wrap, pressing down to cling to food. Apply board lid. Freeze.

Reheating Instructions

Defrost in refrigerator. Remove board lid and plastic wrap. Transfer to saucepan or microwave safe dish and heat thoroughly. Serve over rice.

Divide and Conquer

- Strategize batch sizes based on available containers/cookware.
- Cube beef.
- Brown beef.
- Peel and mince ginger.
- Slice and dice peppers.
- Clean and slice mushrooms.
- Prepare and label all packaging.

Microwave garlic cloves 8 to 10 seconds and the skin will be easy to remove. One clove of garlic is equivalent to ½ teaspoon minced garlic. While fresh is preferred, some recipe quantities make jarred, minced garlic a very attractive option!

Citrus Glazed Corned Beef

Makes 6, 12, or 18 4-serving meals

(approximately ¾ cup per serving)

Recommended Packaging

aluminum tins with board lids
plastic wrap

Ingredients and Instructions

6 meals 24 servings	12 meals 48 servings	18 meals 72 servings	
12 pounds	**24 pounds**	**36 pounds**	**corned beef brisket**

Boil corned beef. See *Preparing Beef.*

Citrus Glaze

4 cups	**8 cups**	**12 cups**	**red currant jelly**
1 cup	**2 cups**	**3 cups**	**Port wine**
2 tablespoons	**¼ cup**	**6 tablespoons**	**orange zest**
3 tablespoons	**6 tablespoons**	**9 tablespoons**	**lemon zest**
½ cup	**1 cup**	**1½ cups**	**fresh orange juice**
½ cup	**1 cup**	**1½ cups**	**fresh lemon juice**
1 cup	**2 cups**	**3 cups**	**shallots, finely chopped**
2 tablespoons	**¼ cup**	**6 tablespoons**	**dry mustard**
1 tablespoon	**2 tablespoons**	**3 tablespoons**	**ground ginger**
1 tablespoon	**2 tablespoons**	**3 tablespoons**	**ground black pepper**
1 teaspoon	**2 teaspoons**	**1 tablespoon**	**salt**

Preheat oven to 350°. Work in batches as necessary. In a stockpot over medium-low heat, combine all ingredients. Cook, stirring frequently, until jelly melts. Remove pan from heat and let sauce stand. Remove corned beef briskets from boiling pans and place them in shallow roasting pans, fat side up. Remove excess fat.

Divide and Conquer

- Strategize batch sizes based on available containers/cookware.
- Boil beef and remove fat.
- Prepare sauce.
- Prepare and label all packaging.

| cup | 2 cups | 3 cups | whole grain mustard |
| cup | 2 cups | 3 cups | dark brown sugar, packed |

laze briskets in batches as necessary. Using a spatula, divide and spread mustard evenly over briskets. Divide sauce and pour over briskets. rinkle with brown sugar. Place roasting pans in oven and bake, basting every 15 minutes, until corned beef is glazed (approximately 45 inutes). Remove briskets, reserving sauce. Slice on the diagonal, perpendicular to the grain. Divide evenly among tins. Cover with citrus ize, dividing evenly among tins. Cool. Cover with a sheet of plastic wrap, pressing down to cling to food. Apply board lid. Freeze.

Reheating Instructions

efrost in refrigerator. Remove board lid and plastic wrap. Transfer to microwave safe dish. Cover and warm. Serve with a family favorite otato and vegetable.

Peeling an orange, or juicing a lemon? Take a few minutes to remove the zest. Bag and freeze. You'll have some wonderful flavor on hand to add to cookie dough, pound cakes, and pies. And it's a great way to stock up for recipes like Citrus Glazed Corned Beef.

Divide and Conquer

- ✆ Strategize batch sizes based on available containers/cookware.
- ✆ Cube beef.
- ✆ Brown beef.
- ✆ Chop and sauté onions.
- ✆ Peel and cut carrots.
- ✆ Prepare and label all packaging.

A scaled 2-quart pitcher makes a great large-quantity measuring cup!

Irish Beef Stew

Makes 6, 12, or 18 4-serving meals

(approximately 1½ cups per serving)

Recommended Packaging

aluminum tins with board lids
plastic wrap

Ingredients and Instructions

6 meals 24 servings	12 meals 48 servings	18 meals 72 servings	
			olive or vegetable oil
12 pounds	**24 pounds**	**36 pounds**	**beef cut into 1-inch chunks** **salt and pepper**

Work in batches as necessary. In a large skillet or Dutch oven over medium-high heat, heat oil. Season and brown beef chunks. Refrigerate. Reserve meat juices and reduce to taste.

			olive or vegetable oil
3	**6**	**9**	**medium onions, chopped**
2 tablespoons	**¼ cup**	**6 tablespoons**	**garlic, pressed or minced**
18 cups	**36 cups**	**54 cups**	**beef stock or canned broth (include reserved** **meat juices)**
11 ounces	**22 ounces**	**33 ounces**	**tomato paste**
6 tablespoons	**¾ cup**	**1 cup plus** **2 tablespoons**	**Worcestershire sauce**
2 tablespoons	**¼ cup**	**6 tablespoons**	**sugar**
2 tablespoons	**¼ cup**	**6 tablespoons**	**dried thyme**
8	**16**	**24**	**bay leaves**

Work in batches as necessary. In a large stockpot over medium heat, heat oil. Sauté onions and garlic until tender. Stir in beef stock or canned broth, tomato paste, Worcestershire sauce, sugar, thyme, and bay leaves and bring to a boil at high heat. Add browned beef chunks. Reduce heat, cover, and simmer until meat is tender (approximately 2 to 2½ hours). Remove and discard bay leaves.

1 pound	**2 pounds**	**3 pounds**	**carrots, cut into 1-inch pieces**
8	**16**	**24**	**medium potatoes, peeled and cubed** **salt and pepper to taste**

Add carrots and simmer 15 minutes. Add potatoes and simmer 15 more minutes (potatoes should be slightly undercooked). Season with salt and pepper. Remove from heat. Divide evenly among tins. Cool. Cover with a sheet of plastic wrap, pressing down to cling to food. Apply board lid. Freeze.

Reheating Instructions

Defrost in refrigerator. Remove board lid and plastic wrap. Transfer to saucepan or microwave safe dish and heat thoroughly.

Italian Swiss Steak

Makes 6, 12, or 18 4-serving meals
(approximately 1 cup per serving)

Divide and Conquer
- Strategize batch sizes based on available containers/cookware.
- Trim fat from beef and cut into individually-sized portions.
- Chop and sauté onions.
- Prepare and label all packaging.

ecommended Packaging

aluminum tins with board lids
plastic wrap

gredients and Instructions

meals servings	12 meals 48 servings	18 meals 72 servings	
pounds	24 pounds	36 pounds	round steak, visible fat trimmed
			olive or vegetable oil
cups	3 cups	4½ cups	all-purpose flour
ablespoon	2 tablespoons	3 tablespoons	salt
easpoon	2 teaspoons	1 tablespoon	ground black pepper

t round steak into individually-sized portions. Work in batches as necessary. In a large baking dish, thoroughly combine flour, salt, and pper. In a large skillet or Dutch oven over medium-high heat, heat oil. Dredge beef pieces in seasoned flour and brown both sides. move from pan. Refrigerate.

	8	12	olive or vegetable oil medium onions, chopped
pounds	14 pounds	21 pounds	canned diced tomatoes, undrained
ablespoons	¼ cup	6 tablespoons	dried thyme
ablespoons	¼ cup	6 tablespoons	dried oregano
ablespoons	¼ cup	6 tablespoons	dried basil
ablespoon	2 tablespoons	3 tablespoons	salt

heat oven to 350°. Work in batches as necessary. Using the same skillet over medium heat, heat oil. Sauté onions until tender. Transfer ons and browned steak pieces to a large Dutch oven or roaster. Add tomatoes and spices, stirring to combine. Cover and bake until at is tender (approximately 2 to 2½ hours). Remove from oven. Remove any fat from the surface of the liquid. Divide meat and sauce nly among tins. Cool. Cover with a sheet of plastic wrap, pressing down to cling to food. Apply board lid. Freeze.

eheating Instructions

frost in refrigerator. Remove board lid and plastic wrap. Transfer to microwave safe dish and heat thoroughly.

Divide and Conquer

- Strategize batch sizes based on available containers/cookware.
- Prepare dredging mixture.
- Cube beef.
- Brown beef.
- Chop and sauté vegetables.
- Prepare and label all packaging.

Your food exchange group can adopt a food co-op strategy. Purchase spices in bulk from a restaurant-supply store or bulk warehouse. Divide among members of your group and realize radical savings!

Moroccan Beef

Makes 6, 12, or 18 4-serving meals

(approximately 1 cup per serving)

Recommended Packaging

aluminum tins with board lids
plastic wrap

Ingredients and Instructions

6 meals	12 meals	18 meals	
24 servings	48 servings	72 servings	
			olive oil
8 pounds	16 pounds	24 pounds	beef, cut into 1-inch chunks
1 cup	2 cups	3 cups	all-purpose flour
3 tablespoons	6 tablespoons	9 tablespoons	ground cumin
3 tablespoons	6 tablespoons	9 tablespoons	ground oregano
5 teaspoons	3 tablespoons plus 1 teaspoon	5 tablespoons	ground allspice
1 teaspoon	2 teaspoons	1 tablespoon	cayenne pepper
2 tablespoons	¼ cup	6 tablespoons	salt

Work in batches as necessary. In a large baking dish, thoroughly combine flour, spices, and salt. In a large skillet or Dutch oven over medium-high heat, heat oil. Dredge beef chunks in flour and spice mixture and brown. Transfer to a large bowl. Refrigerate.

			olive or vegetable oil
3	6	9	large onions, chopped
3 pounds	6 pounds	9 pounds	carrots, sliced into ¼-inch slices

Work in batches as necessary. Using the same skillet over medium heat, heat oil. Sauté onions, carrots, and garlic until tender. Remove from pan and set aside.

30 ounces	60 ounces	90 ounces	tomato paste
2¾ cups	5½ cups	8¼ cups	orange juice
1 cup	2 cups	3 cups	red wine vinegar
4 cups	8 cups	12 cups	beef stock or canned broth
⅔ cup	1⅓ cup	2 cups	sugar
3 tablespoons	6 tablespoons	9 tablespoons	garlic, minced or pressed

Preheat oven to 350°. Place tomato paste, orange juice, vinegar, beef stock or canned broth, sugar, and garlic into a large roaster, stirring to combine. Add beef chunks and onion mixture. Cover and bake, stirring occasionally, until beef is tender (approximately 2 hours). Remove from oven. Divide evenly among tins. Cool. Cover with a sheet of plastic wrap, pressing down to cling to food. Apply board lid. Freeze.

Reheating Instructions

Defrost in refrigerator. Remove board lid and plastic wrap. Transfer to saucepan or microwave safe dish and heat thoroughly.

Roast Barbecue

Makes 6, 12, or 18 4-serving meals

(approximately 1 cup per serving)

Recommended Packaging
aluminum tins with board lids
plastic wrap

Ingredients and Instructions

6 meals / 24 servings	12 meals / 48 servings	18 meals / 72 servings	
			olive or vegetable oil
12 pounds	24 pounds	36 pounds	English shoulder or chuck roast

Preheat oven to 350°. In a large skillet or Dutch oven over medium-high heat, heat oil. Individually brown roasts on all sides and transfer to large roasters.

6 meals / 24 servings	12 meals / 48 servings	18 meals / 72 servings	
	6	9	large onions, chopped
tablespoons	¾ cup	1 cup plus 2 tablespoons	vinegar
tablespoons	¾ cup	1 cup plus 2 tablespoons	fresh lemon juice
¼ cups	4½ cups	6¾ cups	water
	12	18	celery ribs, chopped
cups	12 cups	18 cups	ketchup
cup	1 cup	1½ cups	Worcestershire sauce
tablespoons	¾ cup	1 cup plus 2 tablespoons	brown sugar, packed
tablespoons	6 tablespoons	9 tablespoons	prepared mustard
tablespoons	¾ cup	1 cup plus 2 tablespoons	chili powder
teaspoons	4 teaspoons	2 tablespoons	ground black pepper

In a large container, mix ingredients. Pour over chuck roasts. Cover and roast approximately 3 hours. Remove beef and shred with a fork, removing any fat or gristle. Return shredded beef to sauce and continue roasting until meat is very tender (approximately 2 more hours). Divide evenly among tins. Cool. Cover with a sheet of plastic wrap, pressing down to cling to food. Apply board lid. Freeze.

Reheating Instructions

Defrost in refrigerator. Remove board lid and plastic wrap. Transfer to saucepan or microwave safe dish and heat thoroughly. Serve as a sandwich or baked potato filling.

Divide and Conquer

- Strategize batch sizes based on available containers/cookware.
- Chop vegetables.
- Prepare and label all packaging.

Consider purchasing a large electrical roaster, dividing the cost among group members. Plan cooking schedules to share the roaster among those who'll need it!

Orange Beef

Makes 6, 12, or 18 4-serving meals

(approximately 1 cup per serving)

Recommended Packaging

aluminum tins with board lids

plastic wrap

6 meals	12 meals	18 meals	
24 servings	48 servings	72 servings	

Shopping List

10 pounds	20 pounds	30 pounds	round steak or better, sliced very thin perpendicular to the grain
6 cups	12 cups	18 cups	broccoli florets
¾ cup	1½ cups	2¼ cups	peanut oil
4	6	8	oranges, zest removed and oranges reserved for another use
4 teaspoons	8 teaspoons	¼ cup	garlic, pressed or minced
4 teaspoons	8 teaspoons	¼ cup	ground ginger
2 cups	4 cups	6 cups	soy sauce
1 cup	2 cups	3 cups	corn starch
8 cups	16 cups	24 cups	beef stock or canned broth
2 cups	4 cups	6 cups	sherry
3 cups	6 cups	9 cups	orange marmalade
1 teaspoon	2 teaspoons	1 tablespoon	red pepper flakes

Instructions

6 cups	12 cups	18 cups	broccoli florets

Steam broccoli until tender crisp. Divide evenly among tins (approximately 1 cup per meal or ¼ cup per serving).

Prepare 2 batches of the following:	Prepare 4 batches of the following:	Prepare 6 batches of the following:	
1 cup			soy sauce
½ cup			corn starch
4 cups			beef stock or canned broth
1 cup			sherry
1½ cups			orange marmalade
½ teaspoon			red pepper flakes

- Slice beef into thin strips.
- Clean and chop broccoli.
- Steam broccoli.
- Mix sauce batches.
- Prepare and label all packaging.

Prepare enough batches for desired yield. Whisk together soy sauce, cornstarch, beef stock or canned broth, sherry, marmalade, and red pepper (each batch in a separate container). Set aside.

5 pounds	**round steak or better, sliced very thin perpendicular to the grain**
2 tablespoons	**peanut oil**
2 oranges	**orange zest removed**
2 teaspoons	**garlic, pressed or minced**
2 teaspoons	**ground ginger**

Prepare enough batches for desired yield. In a wok or large skillet over medium-high heat, heat oil. Add beef strips and stir-fry. Add orange zest, garlic, and ginger. Stir-fry 1 more minute. Stir a batch of sauce into beef and simmer until thickened. Divide evenly among tins (approximately 3 cups per meal or ¾ cup per serving), pouring over broccoli. Repeat with remaining batches. Cool. Cover each tin with a sheet of plastic wrap, pressing down to cling to food. Apply board lid. Freeze.

Reheating Instructions

Defrost in refrigerator. Remove board lid and plastic wrap. Transfer to saucepan or microwave safe dish and reheat thoroughly. Serve with rice.

Slicing beef while partially frozen allows for easy, ultra-thin slices!

Roast Beef with Carrots

Makes 6, 12, or 18 4-serving meals

(approximately 1 cup per serving)

Divide and Conquer

- Strategize batch sizes based on available containers/cookware.
- Chop vegetables.
- Cook carrots.
- Prepare and label all packaging.

Recommended Packaging

aluminum tins with board lids
plastic wrap

Ingredients and Instructions

6 meals	12 meals	18 meals	
24 servings	48 servings	72 servings	
			olive or vegetable oil
12 pounds	24 pounds	36 pounds	lean beef roast
			salt and pepper

Preheat oven to 350°. Work in batches as necessary. In a large skillet or Dutch oven over high heat, heat oil. Season and brown roasts on all sides and transfer to large roasters.

			olive or vegetable oil
3	6	9	medium onions, finely chopped
1 pound	2 pounds	3 pounds	carrots, finely chopped
8	16	24	celery ribs, finely chopped
6	12	18	bay leaves
2 tablespoons	¼ cup	6 tablespoons	dried thyme
9 cups	18 cups	27 cups	beef stock or canned broth

Work in batches as necessary. Using the same skillet over medium heat, heat oil. Sauté onions, carrots, and celery until onions are golden. Add vegetable mixture, bay leaves, and thyme to roasters. Pour beef stock or canned broth over roasts and vegetables. Cover and roast until tender (approximately 3 to 3½ hours). Remove meat from roasters. Let meat stand, covered, at least 10 minutes before slicing. Remove any fat from the surface of the liquid. Strain the stock and discard vegetables and bay leaves. Reserve stock to prepare gravy.

| 3 pounds | 6 pounds | 9 pounds | carrots, cut into 2-inch pieces |

Cook carrots in a stockpot containing boiling water until tender, yet firm. Drain. Set aside.

| ¾ cup | 1½ cups | 2¼ cups | butter, melted |
| ¾ cup | 1½ cups | 2¼ cups | all-purpose flour |

In a large skillet over medium heat, melt butter. Stir in flour and cook 3 to 5 minutes. Slowly add reserved stock, stirring constantly until well blended. Whisk over medium heat until thickened. Remove from stove. Slice roasts and divide evenly among tins. Divide carrots evenly among tins. Pour gravy over meat and carrots, dividing evenly among tins. Cool. Cover with a sheet of plastic wrap, pressing down to cling to food. Apply board lid. Freeze.

Reheating Instructions

Defrost in refrigerator. Remove board lid and plastic wrap. Transfer to microwave safe dish and heat thoroughly. Serve with mashed or baked potatoes.

Easily remove fat from sauces and stocks by refrigerating until liquid congeals. Fat can be quickly skimmed from top.

Rueben Loaf Kits

Makes 6, 12, or 18 4-serving meals

(¼ loaf per serving)

Recommended Packaging

one gallon freezer bags
snack bags
plastic wrap

Ingredients and Instructions

| 6 meals | 12 meals | 18 meals | |
24 servings	48 servings	72 servings	
6	12	18	one pound loaves frozen bread dough

Wrap each loaf of dough in freezer foil or plastic wrap.

6 cups	12 cups	18 cups	cubed or sliced cooked corned beef
6 cups	12 cups	18 cups	shredded Swiss cheese
3 pounds	6 pounds	9 pounds	sauerkraut
1½ cups	3 cups	4½ cups	Thousand Island dressing (or individual 1.5 ounce dressing packets)

Package corned beef in snack bags (1 cup per loaf). Package cheese in snack bags (1 cup per loaf). Package sauerkraut in ½ pound portions in snack bags (generous 1 cup per loaf). Package Thousand Island dressing in ¼ cup quantities. Place a loaf of frozen bread, a package of corned beef, a package of cheese, and a package of sauerkraut in each one gallon freezer bag. Include the following preparation instructions. Seal bag, pressing out excess air. Freeze. Furnish Thousand Island salad dressing separately (do not freeze).

Preparation Instructions

Remove bread from wrapping. Thaw in refrigerator (approximately 6 hours) and then set out to rise (approximately 1 to 2 hours). Or, thaw on counter (approximately 5 hours). Look for dough to double in bulk. Defrost cheese, sauerkraut, and corned beef in refrigerator. Drain sauerkraut and corned beef well. Roll dough to approximately 10-inch x 14-inch. Scatter corned beef down center of dough. Drizzle Thousand Island dressing over corned beef. Top with half of cheese. Top with half of sauerkraut. Repeat with second layer of cheese and sauerkraut. Using a knife, cut strips in dough on either side of filling. Alternating side to side, pull strips decoratively over filling (pinch end strips to seal). Cover and allow to rise again (approximately 45 minutes). Preheat oven to 350°. Bake approximately 40 minutes. If bread browns too quickly, cover with foil to halt browning.

Divide and Conquer

- Strategize batch sizes based on available containers/cookware.
- Cook corned beef.
- Cube corned beef.
- Package meat.
- Package frozen dough.
- Package cheese.
- Package sauerkraut.
- Package dressing.
- Prepare and label all packaging.

Frozen entrées might be an appetizer in disguise. Consider how your entrées might be adapted to small portions and served as a starter. Convert Country Meatloaf to meatballs or mini burgers. Serve Roast Barbecue or Sloppy Joes on mini corn muffins. Prepare loaves in a long, thin strip. Slice for nearly bite-sized pieces.

South African Beef Stew

Makes 6, 12, or 18 4-serving meals

(approximately 1½ cups per serving)

Divide and Conquer

- Strategize batch sizes based on available containers/cookware.
- Cube beef.
- Chop and sauté onions.
- Peel and mince ginger.
- Peel and cut carrots.
- Premeasure and combine seasonings.
- Prepare and label all packaging.

When freezing potatoes for future reheating, slightly undercook.

Recommended Packaging

aluminum tins with board lids
plastic wrap

Ingredients and Instructions

6 meals 24 servings	12 meals 48 servings	18 meals 72 servings	
			olive or vegetable oil
6	12	18	medium onions, chopped
72 ounces	9 pounds	13 lbs 5 oz	canned diced tomatoes, undrained
¼ cup	½ cup	¾ cup	fresh ginger, minced
2 tablespoons	¼ cup	6 tablespoons	garlic, pressed or minced
9	18	27	cinnamon sticks
4½ tablespoons	9 tablespoons	13½ tablespoons	curry powder
7 teaspoons	4 tablespoons plus 2 teaspoons	7 tablespoons	ground coriander
7 teaspoons	4 tablespoons plus 2 teaspoons	7 tablespoons	ground cumin
7 teaspoons	4 tablespoons plus 2 teaspoons	7 tablespoons	fennel seed
1 tablespoon	2 tablespoons	3 tablespoons	cardamom
2 teaspoons	4 teaspoons	2 tablespoons	cayenne pepper
12 pounds	24 pounds	36 pounds	beef cut into 1-inch chunks
2 cups	4 cups	6 cups	water
1 tablespoon	2 tablespoons	3 tablespoons	salt

Work in batches as necessary. In a large stockpot over medium heat, heat oil. Sauté onions until tender. Add tomatoes, garlic, and ginger and cook 5 minutes, stirring occasionally. Stir in cinnamon sticks, curry powder, coriander, cumin, fennel seed, cardamom, and cayenne pepper. Continue stirring and simmering 5 more minutes. Add beef chunks, water, and salt. Bring to a boil. Reduce heat, cover, and simmer until beef is almost tender (approximately 2 to 2½ hours).

1 pound	2 pounds	3 pounds	carrots, cut into 1-inch pieces
8	16	24	potatoes, peeled and cubed

Add carrots and simmer 15 minutes. Add potatoes and simmer 15 more minutes (potatoes should be slightly undercooked). Remove from heat. Divide evenly among tins. Cool. Cover with a sheet of plastic wrap, pressing down to cling to food. Apply board lid. Freeze.

Reheating Instructions

Defrost in refrigerator. Remove board lid and plastic wrap. Transfer to saucepan or microwave safe dish and heat thoroughly.

Ground Beef

Beefy Three Cheese Enchiladas
Country Meat Loaf
Lasagna
Meatballs
Pizza Burger Kits
Sloppy Joes
South of the Border Lasagna
Spaghetti Meat Sauce
Taco or Burrito Kits

Some food items are more easily assembled or packaged when chilled. Chill Beefy Three Cheese Enchilada filling to make spoon-filling the tortillas a breeze!

Beefy Three Cheese Enchiladas

Makes 6, 12, or 18 4-serving meals

(approximately 1½ enchiladas per serving)

Recommended Packaging

aluminum tins with board lids
snack bags
plastic wrap

Ingredients and Instructions

6 meals 24 servings	12 meals 48 servings	18 meals 72 servings	
3 pounds	6 pounds	9 pounds	lean ground beef
2 tablespoons	¼ cup	6 tablespoons	garlic, pressed or minced
2 tablespoons	¼ cup	6 tablespoons	ground cumin
1 tablespoon	2 tablespoons	3 tablespoons	chili powder
48 ounces	96 ounces	9 pounds	mild salsa or picante sauce
1½ pounds	3 pounds	4½ pounds	cream cheese, softened and cut into chunks
6 cups	12 cups	18 cups	shredded cheddar cheese
6 cups	12 cups	18 cups	shredded Monterey Jack cheese
3	6	9	red or green peppers, finely chopped

Work in batches as necessary. In a large stockpot over medium heat, brown ground beef. Drain and return to pan. Over medium heat add garlic, cumin, chili powder, and salsa, stirring to combine. When mixture is heated, add cream cheese chunks, stirring until melted. Stir in shredded cheeses and chopped peppers. Remove from heat and set aside.

48 ounces	96 ounces	9 pounds	mild salsa or picante sauce
4½ cups	9 cups	13½ cups	shredded cheddar or Monterey Jack cheese
36	72	108	6-inch flour tortillas

Package salsa or picante sauce in snack bags (1 cup per meal or ¼ cup per serving). Package cheese in snack bags (¾ cup per meal or 3 tablespoons per serving). Assemble enchiladas by placing ½ cup beef and cheese mixture onto each tortilla and rolling. Place 6 enchiladas (or 1½ per serving) in each tin. Cover with a sheet of plastic wrap, pressing down to cling to food. Place a package of salsa and a package of cheese in each tin. Apply board lid. Freeze.

Reheating Instructions

Defrost in refrigerator. Preheat oven to 350°. Remove board lid, salsa, cheese, and plastic wrap. Transfer to baking dish, if desired, or bake in aluminum tin. Spread salsa over enchiladas. Cover loosely with foil to prevent drying. Bake until bubbly around the edges and hot in the center (approximately 30 minutes). Remove foil and sprinkle with cheese during last 5 minutes of baking. Let stand at room temperature 15 minutes before serving.

Country Meat Loaf

Makes 6, 12, or 18 4-serving meals

(approximately 1 cup per serving)

Recommended Packaging

aluminum tins with board lids

plastic wrap

Ingredients and Instructions

6 meals 24 servings	12 meals 48 servings	18 meals 72 servings	
			olive or vegetable oil
3	6	9	large onions, finely chopped
1 tablespoon	2 tablespoons	3 tablespoons	garlic, pressed or minced

Work in batches as necessary. In a large skillet over medium heat, heat oil. Sauté onions and garlic until tender. Remove from heat and set aside. Cool.

9 pounds	18 pounds	27 pounds	lean ground beef
3 cups	6 cups	9 cups	oatmeal
6	12	18	eggs, lightly beaten
1½ cups	3 cups	4½ cups	ketchup, divided
1½ cups	3 cups	4½ cups	chili sauce, divided
1 tablespoon	2 tablespoons	3 tablespoons	salt
1½ teaspoons	1 tablespoon	4½ teaspoons	ground black pepper

Using gloved hands, in a large bowl combine ground beef, oatmeal, and cooled onion/garlic mixture. In another bowl, whisk together eggs, half of ketchup, half of chili sauce, salt, and pepper. Pour egg mixture over beef mixture. Mix ingredients together, handling just enough to combine evenly. Lightly spray each tin with a nonstick spray. Divide evenly among tins. Divide and spread remaining half of ketchup and chili sauce over each loaf. Cover with a sheet of plastic wrap, pressing down to cling to food. Apply board lid. Freeze.

Reheating Instructions

Defrost in refrigerator. Preheat oven to 375°. Remove board lid and plastic wrap. Bake until the loaf has begun to shrink from the sides of the pan (approximately 1 hour). Transfer to a rack and let stand 10 minutes before cutting.

Divide and Conquer

- ✎ Strategize batch sizes based on available containers/cookware.
- ✎ Chop and sauté vegetables.
- ✎ Prepare and label all packaging.

Meatloaf can be frozen baked or unbaked. An unbaked meatloaf provides lots of possibilities! It can be prepared for a comforting, cozy meal, transformed into meatballs (with many different sauce possibilities), or formed into patties and grilled for burgers.

Lasagna

Makes 6, 12, or 18 4-serving meals

(Approximately 1½ cups per serving)

Recommended Packaging

5"x12" or 8"x 8" (6-cup) aluminum tins
with board lids
snack bags
plastic wrap

Ingredients and Instructions

6 meals 24 servings	12 meals 48 servings	18 meals 72 servings	
4½ pounds	9 pounds	13½ pounds	lean ground beef salt and pepper

Work in batches as necessary. In a large skillet or Dutch oven over medium heat, season and brown ground beef, stirring often to break up clumps. Drain. Refrigerate.

2	4	6	medium onions, finely chopped
1½ teaspoons	1 tablespoon	4½ teaspoons	garlic, pressed or minced
5 tablespoons	½ cup plus 2 tablespoons	¾ cup plus 3 tablespoons	dried parsley
1½ tablespoons	3 tablespoons	4½ tablespoons	dried basil
1 tablespoon	2 tablespoons	3 tablespoons	dried oregano
6	12	18	bay leaves
1 teaspoon	2 teaspoons	1 tablespoon	ground black pepper
72 ounces	9 pounds	13 lbs 8 oz	canned tomato sauce
24 ounces	48 ounces	72 ounces	canned chopped tomatoes, undrained

Place all ingredients in a large stockpot. Cover and bring to a boil. Uncover, reduce heat, and simmer, stirring occasionally, 1 hour. Reserve 1 cup (or ¼ cup per serving) tomato sauce per tin in a separate container for later use in assembling lasagna. Stir browned beef into remaining sauce.

Size Adjuster (9" x 13")

Reserve 1½ cups (or ¼ cup per serving) tomato sauce per tin in a separate container for later use in assembling lasagna. Stir browned beef into remaining sauce.

4½ pounds	9 pounds	13½ pounds	ricotta cheese
9 cups	18 cups	27 cups	shredded mozzarella cheese

Divide and Conquer

- ☞ Strategize batch sizes based on available containers/cookware.
- ☞ Brown and drain ground beef.
- ☞ Prepare tomato sauce.
- ☞ Assemble cheese and egg filling.
- ☞ Package cheese.
- ☞ Prepare and label all packaging.

| ½ cups | 3 cups | 4½ cups | shredded Parmesan cheese |
| | 18 | 27 | eggs, lightly beaten |

n a large bowl, thoroughly combine cheeses and eggs. Set aside.

| ½ cups | 3 cups | 4½ cups | shredded Parmesan cheese |

Package cheese in snack bags (¼ cup per meal or 1 tablespoon per serving).

Size Adjuster (9" x 13")

Package cheese in snack bags (6 tablespoons per meal or 1 tablespoon per serving).

| 6 | 72 | 108 | lasagna noodles, slightly undercooked |
| cups | 12 cups | 18 cups | reserved tomato sauce |

Lightly spray a tin with nonstick cooking spray. Spread ½ cup (or 2 tablespoons per serving) of reserved tomato sauce on bottom of tin. Cover sauce with a layer of noodles. Divide and spread half of cheese and egg mixture evenly among tins. Divide and spread half of tomato and meat sauce evenly among tins. Cover with a layer of noodles. Repeat. Spread ½ cup (or 2 tablespoons per serving) of reserved tomato sauce over noodles. Cover with a sheet of plastic wrap, pressing down to cling to food. Place one package of cheese in each tin. Apply board lid. Freeze.

Size Adjuster (9" x 13")

Lightly spray each tin with nonstick cooking spray. Spread ¾ cup (or 2 tablespoons per serving) of reserved tomato sauce on bottom of each tin. Cover sauce with a layer of noodles. Divide and spread half of cheese and egg mixture evenly among tins. Divide and spread half of tomato and meat sauce evenly among tins. Repeat. Spread ¾ cup (or 2 tablespoons per serving) of reserved tomato sauce over noodles. Cover with a sheet of plastic wrap, pressing down to cling to food. Place one package of cheese in each tin. Apply board lid. Freeze.

Reheating Instructions

Defrost in refrigerator. Preheat oven to 350°. Remove board lid, cheese, and plastic wrap. Cover loosely with foil to prevent drying. Bake until bubbly around the edges and hot in center (approximately 30 to 40 minutes). Remove foil and sprinkle with Parmesan cheese during last 5 minutes of baking. Let stand 15 minutes before cutting.

Size Adjuster

6 Meal Equivalents	12 Meal Equivalents	18 Meal Equivalents
(6) 5" x 12" or 8" x 8"	(12) 5" x 12" or 8" x 8"	(18) 5" x 12" or 8" x 8"
(4) 9" x 13"	(8) 9" x 13"	(12) 9" x 13"

Meatballs

Makes 6, 12, or 18 4-serving meals

(approximately 6 meatballs per serving)

Recommended Packaging

aluminum tins with board lids

plastic wrap

Ingredients and Instructions

6 meals 24 servings	12 meals 48 servings	18 meals 72 servings	
27 slices	54 slices	81 slices	bread, cut into small cubes
½ cup	1 cup	1½ cups	dried parsley
2	4	6	medium onions, finely chopped
5 teaspoons	10 teaspoons	5 tablespoons	garlic, pressed or minced
2 cups	4 cups	6 cups	milk
18	36	54	eggs, lightly beaten
2 tablespoons	¼ cup	6 tablespoons	salt
1 teaspoon	2 teaspoons	1 tablespoon	ground black pepper
9 pounds	18 pounds	27 pounds	lean ground beef

Using gloved hands, in a large bowl combine bread cubes, parsley, onions, garlic, milk, eggs, salt, and pepper. Mix thoroughly. Add ground beef. Mix ingredients together, handling just enough to combine evenly. Shape into approximate 1½-inch balls. Work in batches as necessary. In a medium nonstick frying pan over medium heat, add meatballs and brown on all sides. Transfer cooked meatballs to paper towel lined plate and pat gently to remove excess oil. Alternatively, place meatballs on a foil-lined cookie sheet and bake 20 minutes at 375º, turning once. Meatballs should be lightly browned and no longer pink in the center. Divide evenly among tins (approximately 6 meatballs per serving). Cover with a sheet of plastic wrap, pressing down to cling to food. Apply board lid. Attach a bag of sauce if desired. Freeze.

Reheating Instructions

Defrost in refrigerator. Preheat oven to 350°. Remove board lid and plastic wrap. Add preferred sauce and bake 30 minutes.

Spaghetti Sauce
(approximately 12 cups)

2	medium onions, finely chopped
1½ teaspoons	garlic, pressed or minced
5 tablespoons	dried parsley
1½ tablespoons	dried basil
1 tablespoon	dried oregano
6	bay leaves

Divide and Conquer

- Strategize batch sizes based on available containers/cookware.
- Cube bread.
- Chop and sauté onions.
- Prepare sauces as desired.
- Prepare and label all packaging.

teaspoon	ground black pepper
2 ounces	canned tomato sauce
4 ounces	canned chopped tomatoes, undrained

Place all ingredients in a large stockpot. Cover and bring to a boil. Uncover, reduce heat, and simmer, stirring occasionally, for 1 hour. Remove and discard bay leaves. Cool. Divide evenly among freezer bags (½ cup per serving). Seal bag, pressing out excess air. Freeze.

Beef Gravy
(approximately 12 cups)

¼ cup	butter
¼ cup	all-purpose flour
2 cups	beef stock or canned broth
½ cups	heavy cream
	salt and pepper to taste

In a large stockpot over medium heat, melt butter. Stir in flour and cook 3 to 5 minutes. Slowly add beef stock or canned broth, stirring constantly until well blended. Whisk over medium heat until thickened. Stir in cream. Season with salt and pepper. Cool. Divide evenly among freezer bags (½ cup per serving). Seal bag, pressing out excess air. Freeze.

Sweet and Sour Sauce
(approximately 12 cups)

4 ounces	Italian-style stewed tomatoes
cups	beef stock or canned broth
cup	onion, finely chopped
cup	brown sugar, packed
½ teaspoons	garlic, pressed or minced
tablespoons	fresh lemon juice

In a large stock pot, crush tomatoes with a potato masher. Add beef stock or canned broth, onion, brown sugar, garlic and lemon juice. Bring to a boil. Reduce heat to low and simmer 45 minutes. Cool. Divide evenly among freezer bags (½ cup per serving). Seal bag, pressing out excess air. Freeze.

Evenly portion meatballs by using a melon baller or small ice cream scoop. Or, spread meatballs into an even 1-inch thick square on wax paper. Cut into an even grid of squares. Shape.

Divide and Conquer

- Strategize batch sizes based on available containers/cookware.
- Package English muffins.
- Package cheese slices.
- Prepare and label all packaging.

Consider using latex gloves or rubber gloves when mixing recipe ingredients together by hand. You'll find it easier to stick your hands into a mound of raw ground beef. You will also find that gloves protect your hands when handling hot foods (removing fat and gristle from beef, removing meat from cooked poultry, etc.).

Pizza Burger Kits

Makes 6, 12, or 18 4-serving meals

(1½ burgers per serving)

Recommended Packaging

one gallon freezer bags
foil
plastic wrap

Ingredients and Instructions

| 6 meals | 12 meals | 18 meals | |
24 servings	48 servings	72 servings	
9 pounds	**18 pounds**	**27 pounds**	**lean ground beef**
3 cups	**6 cups**	**9 cups**	**shredded Parmesan cheese**
½	**1**	**1½**	**medium onions, finally chopped**
6 ounces	**12 ounces**	**18 ounces**	**tomato paste**
3 tablespoons	**6 tablespoons**	**9 tablespoons**	**dried basil**
1 tablespoon	**2 tablespoons**	**3 tablespoons**	**dried oregano**
2 teaspoons	**4 teaspoons**	**2 tablespoons**	**salt**
¾ teaspoon	**1½ teaspoons**	**2¼ teaspoons**	**ground black pepper**

In a large bowl combine ground beef, Parmesan cheese, onion, tomato paste, oregano, salt, and pepper. Using gloved hands, mix ingredients together, handling just enough to combine evenly. Divide into patties (approximately 4 ounces each). Individually wrap each burger with plastic wrap. Place 6 wrapped burgers (or 1½ per serving) in each one gallon freezer bag.

| **36** | **72** | **108** | **English muffins, split** |
| **36** | **72** | **108** | **mozzarella cheese slices** |

Wrap English muffins in foil (6 per meal or 1½ per serving). Wrap mozzarella cheese slices in plastic wrap (6 per meal or 1½ per serving). Add a package of English muffins and a package of cheese to each freezer bag containing burgers. Seal bag, pressing out excess air. Freeze.

Reheating Instructions

Defrost burgers in refrigerator. Grill or broil burgers. Toast English muffins. Top each burger with a slice of mozzarella cheese. Top with sliced tomato and a sprinkle of dried basil, if desired.

Sloppy Joes

Makes 6, 12, or 18 4-serving meals

(approximately ¾ cup per serving)

Recommended Packaging — aluminum tins with board lids, plastic wrap

Ingredients and Instructions

6 meals	12 meals	18 meals	
24 servings	48 servings	72 servings	
6 pounds	12 pounds	18 pounds	lean ground beef
			salt and pepper

Work in batches as necessary. In a large skillet or Dutch oven over medium heat, season and brown ground beef, stirring often to break up lumps. Drain. Refrigerate.

6 meals	12 meals	18 meals	
			olive or vegetable oil
6	12	18	medium onions, finely chopped
6	12	18	celery ribs, finely chopped
3	6	9	green bell peppers, seeded and chopped
3 cups	6 cups	9 cups	ketchup
24 ounces	48 ounces	72 ounces	canned tomato sauce
1½ cups	3 cups	4½ cups	water
¾ cup	1½ cups	2¼ cups	red wine vinegar
6 tablespoons	¾ cup	1 cup plus 2 tablespoons	Worcestershire sauce
6 tablespoons	¾ cup	1 cup plus 2 tablespoons	dark brown sugar, packed
1½ tablespoons	3 tablespoons	4½ tablespoons	dried oregano
			salt and pepper to taste
			Tabasco sauce, to taste (optional)

Work in batches as necessary. In a large stockpot over medium heat, heat oil. Sauté onions, celery, and green peppers until tender. Stir in remaining ingredients, including browned beef, and simmer 30 minutes. Season with salt and pepper. Divide evenly among tins. Cool. Cover with a sheet of plastic wrap, pressing down to cling to meat. Apply board lid. Freeze.

Reheating Instructions

Defrost in refrigerator. Remove board lid and plastic wrap. Transfer to saucepan or microwave safe dish and heat thoroughly. Serve as a sandwich or baked potato filling.

Divide and Conquer

- Strategize batch sizes based on available containers/cookware.
- Brown and drain ground beef.
- Chop vegetables.
- Sauté vegetables.
- Prepare and label all packaging.

Surprise an adult crowd by serving kid-friendly sloppy joes, barbeques, or burgers over unexpected breads like cornbread, focaccia, English muffins, or biscuits. Top them off with a great cheese, relish, and/or condiment!

South of the Border Lasagna

Makes 6, 12, or 18 4-serving meals

(approximately 1½ cups per serving)

Recommended Packaging	5" x 12" or 8" x 8" (6-cup) aluminum tins with board lids snack bags plastic wrap

Ingredients and Instructions

6 meals 24 servings	12 meals 48 servings	18 meals 72 servings	
8 pounds	**16 pounds**	**24 pounds**	**lean ground beef** **salt and pepper**

Work in batches as necessary. In a large skillet or Dutch oven over medium heat, season and brown ground beef, stirring often to break up clumps. Drain. Refrigerate.

			olive or vegetable oil
3	**6**	**9**	**medium onions, finely chopped**
1 tablespoon	**2 tablespoons**	**3 tablespoons**	**garlic, pressed or minced**
48 ounces	**96 ounces**	**9 pounds**	**canned tomato sauce**
8 ounces	**16 ounces**	**24 ounces**	**canned chopped mild green chilies**
6 tablespoons	**¾ cup**	**1 cup plus 2 tablespoons**	**chili powder**
4 teaspoons	**8 teaspoons**	**¼ cup**	**salt**

Work in batches as necessary. In a large stockpot over medium heat, heat oil. Sauté onions and garlic until tender. Stir in tomato sauce, green chilies, chili powder, and salt. Simmer 15 minutes. Reserve ½ cup (or 2 tablespoons per serving) tomato sauce per tin in a separate container for later use in assembling lasagna. Set aside. Stir browned beef into remaining sauce. Refrigerate.

Size Adjuster (9" x 13")

Reserve ¾ cup (or 2 tablespoons per serving) tomato sauce per tin in a separate container for later use in assembling lasagna. Set aside. Stir browned beef into remaining sauce. Refrigerate.

---

2 pounds	**4 pounds**	**6 pounds**	**sour cream**
2 pounds	**4 pounds**	**6 pounds**	**cream cheese, softened**
6 cups	**12 cups**	**18 cups**	**shredded Monterey Jack cheese**
4	**8**	**12**	**eggs, beaten**

Divide and Conquer

- Strategize batch sizes based on available containers/cookware.
- Brown and drain ground beef.
- Chop vegetables.
- Sauté vegetables.
- Package cheese.
- Prepare and label all packaging.

In a large bowl, combine sour cream, softened cream cheese, shredded cheese, and eggs. Set aside.

| ½ cups | 9 cups | 13 ½ cups | shredded cheddar cheese |

Package cheese in sandwich bags (¾ cup per meal or 3 tablespoons per serving).

Size Adjuster (9" x 13")

Package cheese in snack bags (1 cup plus 2 tablespoons per meal or 3 tablespoons per serving).

| 8 ounces | 96 ounces | 9 pounds | mild salsa or picante sauce |
| 6 to 40 | 72 to 80 | 108 to 120 | 6-inch soft corn tortillas |

Lightly spray each tin with nonstick cooking spray. Spread ½ cup (or 2 tablespoons per serving) of reserved tomato sauce on bottom of tin. Place a layer of corn tortillas across the bottom of each tin, trimmed to fit as not to overlap. Divide and spread half of meat sauce evenly among tins. Divide and spread half of sour cream and cheese mixture evenly among tins. Cover with a layer of corn tortillas. Repeat. Spread 1 cup salsa (or ¼ cup per serving) over top, covering tortillas completely. Cover with a layer of plastic wrap, pressing down to cling to food. Place a package of cheese in each tin. Apply board lid. Freeze.

Size Adjuster (9" x 13")

Lightly spray each tin with nonstick cooking spray. Spread ¾ cup (or 2 tablespoons per serving) of reserved tomato sauce on bottom of tin. Place a layer of corn tortillas across the bottom of each tin, trimmed to fit as not to overlap. Divide and spread half of meat sauce evenly among tins. Divide and spread half of sour cream and cheese mixture evenly among tins. Cover with a layer of corn tortillas. Repeat. Spread 1½ cups salsa (or ¼ cup per serving) over top, covering tortillas completely. Cover with a layer of plastic wrap, pressing down to cling to food. Place a package of cheese in each tin. Apply board lid. Freeze.

Reheating Instructions

Defrost in refrigerator. Preheat oven to 350°. Remove board lid and plastic wrap. Cover loosely with foil to prevent drying. Bake until bubbly around the edges and hot in center (approximately 30 to 40 minutes). Remove foil and sprinkle with cheese during last 5 minutes of baking. Remove from oven and let stand 15 minutes cutting. Serve with black olives, sour cream, and chopped green onions, as desired.

Size Adjuster		
6 Meal Equivalents	12 Meal Equivalents	18 Meal Equivalents
(6) 5" x 12" or 8" x 8"	(12) 5" x 12" or 8" x 8"	(18) 5" x 12" or 8" x 8"
(4) 9" x 13"	(8) 9" x 13"	(12) 9" x 13"

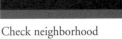

Check neighborhood ethnic stores for tortillas that approach the quality of homemade.

Spaghetti Meat Sauce

Makes 6, 12, or 18 4-serving meals

(approximately 1 cup per serving)

Divide and Conquer

- Strategize batch sizes based on available containers/cookware.
- Brown and drain ground beef.
- Prepare tomato suace.
- Package cheese.
- Prepare and label all packaging.

Send along a bonus with your Spaghetti Meat Sauce. A loaf of garlic bread would be a welcome addition!

Recommended Packaging

aluminum tins with board lids
snack bags
plastic wrap

Ingredients and Instructions

6 meals 24 servings	12 meals 48 servings	18 meals 72 servings	
4½ pounds	9 pounds	13½ pounds	lean ground beef salt and pepper

Work in batches as necessary. In a large skillet or Dutch oven over medium heat, season and brown ground beef, stirring often to break up clumps. Drain. Refrigerate.

2¼ cups	4½ cups	6¾ cups	shredded Parmesan cheese

Package cheese in snack bags (6 tablespoons per meal or 1½ tablespoons per serving).

Tomato Sauce

3	6	9	medium onions, finely chopped
2 teaspoons	4 teaspoons	2 tablespoons	garlic, pressed or minced
6 tablespoons	¾ cup	1 cup plus 2 tablespoons	dried parsley
2½ tablespoons	5 tablespoons	7½ tablespoons	dried basil
1½ tablespoons	3 tablespoons	4½ tablespoons	dried oregano
9	18	27	bay leaves
1½ teaspoons	1 tablespoon	1½ tablespoons	ground black pepper
7 pounds	14 pounds	21 pounds	canned tomato sauce
36 ounces	72 ounces	6 lbs, 12 oz	canned chopped tomatoes, undrained

Place all ingredients in a large stockpot. Cover and bring to a boil. Uncover, reduce heat, and simmer, stirring occasionally, 30 minutes. Remove and discard bay leaves. Stir in browned beef. Simmer 30 more minutes, stirring occasionally. Divide evenly among tins. Cover with a sheet of plastic, pressing down to cling to food. Place a package of cheese in each tin. Apply board lid. Freeze.

Reheating Instructions

Defrost in refrigerator. Remove board lid, cheese, and plastic wrap. Transfer to saucepan or microwave safe dish and heat thoroughly. Serve over spaghetti. Sprinkle with shredded Parmesan cheese.

Taco or Burrito Kits

Makes 6, 12, or 18 4-serving meals

(approximately 2 tacos per serving)

Recommended Packaging

one gallon freezer bags
one quart freezer bags
sandwich bags
snack bags
plastic wrap

Ingredients and Instructions

6 meals 24 servings	12 meals 48 servings	18 meals 72 servings	
6 pounds	12 pounds	18 pounds	lean ground beef
¼ cup	½ cup	¾ cup	chili powder
8 teaspoons	5 tablespoons plus 1 teaspoon	½ cup	onion powder
4 teaspoons	8 teaspoons	¼ cup	ground cumin
4 teaspoons	8 teaspoons	¼ cup	garlic powder
4 teaspoons	8 teaspoons	¼ cup	paprika
4 teaspoons	8 teaspoons	¼ cup	dried oregano
4 teaspoons	8 teaspoons	¼ cup	salt
2 teaspoon	4 teaspoons	2 tablespoons	sugar
3 cups	6 cups	9 cups	water

Work in batches as necessary. In a large skillet or Dutch oven over medium heat, brown ground beef, stirring often to break up clumps. Drain. Return to skillet and add water and spices. Simmer 15 minutes or until water is almost simmered off. Remove from heat. Cool. Divide evenly among one quart freezer bags. Seal bag, pressing out excess air. Refrigerate.

48 ounces 12 cups	96 ounces 24 cups	9 pounds 36 cups	mild salsa or picante sauce shredded cheddar cheese
48	96	144	taco shells or 7-inch to 8-inch flour tortillas

Package salsa or picante sauce in snack bags (1 cup per meal or ¼ cup per serving). Package cheese in sandwich bags (2 cups per meal or ½ cup per serving). Wrap shells or tortillas in plastic wrap (8 tortillas per meal or 2 per serving). Place a package of beef, a package of tortillas, a package of salsa, and a package of cheese in each one gallon freezer bag. Seal bag, pressing out excess air. Freeze.

Reheating Instructions

Defrost in refrigerator. Preheat oven to 350°. Remove packaging. Transfer beef to a baking dish and reheat approximately 15 minutes. Warm tortillas in oven or microwave. Serve with shredded cheese and salsa. Add shredded lettuce, chopped tomatoes, and sour cream, as desired.

Divide and Conquer

- Strategize batch sizes based on available containers/cookware.
- Brown, drain, and season ground beef.
- Package seasoned beef.
- Package salsa or picante sauce.
- Package cheese.
- Package shells or tortillas.
- Prepare and label all packaging.

Express your appreciation to food exchange members by occasionally including a bonus with your entrées! Mexican Bean Dip would be a welcome addition to a Taco or Burrito Kit.

Chicken

Preparing Chicken
African Peanut and Ginger Chicken
Blue Cheese, Walnut, and Mushroom Stuffed Chicken Breasts
Chicken with Artichoke Hearts in a Cream Sauce
Chicken Breasts Chablis
Chicken Breasts in Phyllo
Chicken and Broccoli Quiche
Chicken and Broccoli Loaf Kits
Moroccan Chicken with Apricots and Almonds
Chicken Cordon Bleu with Gruyere Cheese Sauce
Chicken Enchilada Casserole
Chicken Enchiladas with Lime and Cilantro
Chicken Florentine
Chicken Gyro Kits
Chicken Lasagna with Tarragon Cheese Sauce
Chicken Parmigiana
Chicken with Sun Dried Tomatoes in a Cream Sauce
Greek Chicken
Chicken and Vegetable Lasagna with a White Sauce
Coq Au Vin (Chicken in Wine)
Creamed Chicken with Dill and Savory Biscuit Mix
Curried Chicken
Hunan Chicken
White Chicken Chili

(See also Going Beyond Entrée Recipes – Soup's On)

Preparing Chicken

Baking Boneless, Skinless Chicken Breasts

Boneless, skinless chicken breasts
Salt

Preheat oven to 350°. Line a baking sheet with foil. Place breasts on foil in a single layer. Season with salt. Cover with foil. Create a large packet by sealing edges together. Bake until cooked through (approximately 30 to 40 minutes).

Poaching Boneless, Skinless Chicken Breasts

Boneless, skinless chicken breasts
Water
Seasonings (possibilities include white wine, salt, pepper, bay leaves, fresh or dried herbs, carrots, onions, and celery)

In a large skillet, heat to a low simmer enough liquid to barely cover chicken. Add chicken breasts and cook partially covered until the flesh is just firm to the touch (approximately 35 minutes). Maintain a simmer (do not boil). The cooking liquid can be reduced and used for stock.

Roasting Bone-In Chicken Breasts

Large, bone-in, skin-on chicken breasts
Vegetable or olive oil
Salt

Adjust oven racks to middle positions and heat oven to 375°. Rinse chicken well and pat dry. Place chicken breasts on foil-lined baking sheets. Brush with oil and sprinkle generously with salt. Roast until a meat thermometer inserted into thickest part of breast registers 160° (approximately 35 to 40 minutes). If breasts are split, reduce the roasting time by 5 or 10 minutes.

Roasting Whole Chickens

Chicken(s)
Salt and pepper

Adjust oven racks appropriately and heat oven to 350°. Remove giblets from chicken(s) and set aside. Rinse chicken(s) well and pat dry. Season inside and out with salt and pepper (or follow your favorite roasting recipe). Tuck the flap of skin at the neck end under. Place chicken(s) in a roasting pan, preferably on a rack. Add a small amount of liquid (water or broth) to the bottom of the pan. Roast chicken(s) approximately 20 minutes per pound (180° at inner thigh). Baste with pan juices every 20 minutes. Check for doneness by piercing the flesh of the leg with the tip of a knife. If the juices run clear, the chicken is done. You can also check for doneness by twisting the leg. If it moves easily in its socket, the chicken is done.

African Peanut and Ginger Chicken

Makes 6, 12, or 18 4-serving meals

(approximately 1 cup per serving)

Recommended Packaging

aluminum tins with board lids
plastic wrap

Ingredients and Instructions

6 meals	12 meals	18 meals	
24 servings	48 servings	72 servings	
			peanut or vegetable oil
8 pounds	16 pounds	24 pounds	boneless, skinless chicken breasts, cut into bite-sized pieces
½ cup	1 cup	1½ cups	lemon juice
			salt

Work in batches as necessary. Stir lemon juice together with chicken pieces and season with salt. Set aside 10 to 15 minutes. In a large skillet over medium-high heat, heat oil. Add chicken to skillet and sauté, stirring occasionally, until cooked through. Transfer chicken to large bowl, removing batches from skillet with a slotted spoon. Refrigerate. Discard juices.

			peanut or vegetable oil
6	12	18	medium onions, chopped
4	8	12	green bell peppers, seeded and diced
2 tablespoons	¼ cup	6 tablespoons	garlic, pressed or minced
6 tablespoons	¾ cup	1 cup plus 2 tablespoons	fresh ginger, minced
¼ cup	½ cup	¾ cup	chili powder
80 ounces	10 pounds	15 pounds	canned diced tomatoes, slightly drained
4 teaspoons	8 teaspoons	¼ cup	dried thyme
2 teaspoons	4 teaspoons	2 tablespoons	crushed red pepper (or to taste)
2 cups	4 cups	6 cups	natural peanut butter
6 cups	10 cups	15 cups	chicken stock or canned broth

Work in batches as necessary. In a large stockpot over medium heat, heat oil. Sauté onions and green peppers until tender. Add garlic, ginger, and chili powder and cook, stirring constantly, 5 minutes. Stir in tomatoes, thyme, and crushed red pepper. Bring to a simmer and simmer 5 minutes. Add peanut butter and stir until blended evenly. Stir in chicken stock or canned broth and return to simmer. Add cooked chicken. Reduce heat and simmer, stirring frequently, until thickened and reduced (approximately 45 minutes). Remove from heat. Divide evenly among tins. Cool. Cover with a sheet of plastic wrap, pressing down to cling to food. Apply board lid. Freeze.

Reheating Instructions

Defrost in refrigerator. Remove board lid and plastic wrap. Transfer to saucepan or microwave safe dish and heat thoroughly. Serve over rice.

Divide and Conquer

- Strategize batch sizes based on available containers/cookware.
- Cut chicken into bite-sized pieces.
- Cook chicken.
- Peel and mince ginger.
- Chop and sauté vegetables.
- Prepare and label all packaging.

Consider peeling fresh ginger with a vegetable peeler. To chop, thinly slice crosswise and mince.

Blue Cheese, Walnut, and Mushroom Stuffed Chicken Breasts

Makes 6, 12, or 18 4-serving meals

(1 breast per serving)

Recommended Packaging

aluminum tins with board lids
plastic wrap

Ingredients and Instructions

6 meals	12 meals	18 meals
24 servings	48 servings	72 servings

Mushroom Sauce

			olive or vegetable oil
1½ pounds	3 pounds	4½ pounds	mushrooms, sliced
½ cup	1 cup	1½ cups	butter
¼ cup	½ cup	¾ cup	all-purpose flour
3 cups	6 cups	9 cups	chicken stock or canned broth
1 cup	2 cups	3 cups	dry white wine
			salt and pepper to taste

Work in batches as necessary. In a large skillet over medium heat, heat oil. Sauté mushrooms until tender (increase heat if necessary to evaporate liquid). Remove from pan and set aside. Using the same skillet, melt butter over medium heat. Stir in flour and cook 3 to 5 minutes. Slowly add chicken stock or canned broth and wine, stirring constantly until well blended. Whisk over medium heat until thickened. Stir in reserved mushrooms. Season with salt and pepper. Remove from heat and set aside.

			olive or vegetable oil
2	4	6	medium onions, finely chopped
½ pound	1 pound	1½ pounds	mushrooms, finely chopped
12 ounces	24 ounces	36 ounces	blue cheese, crumbled
2 cups	4 cups	6 cups	walnuts, finely chopped

Work in batches as necessary. Using the same skillet over medium heat, heat oil. Sauté onions and mushrooms until tender (increase heat if necessary to evaporate liquid). Transfer to a large bowl. Add crumbed blue cheese and walnuts, stirring until evenly combined. Refrigerate.

10 ounces	20 ounces	30 ounces	breadcrumbs
½ cup	1 cup	1½ cups	walnuts, very finely chopped

In a shallow dish, mix together breadcrumbs and walnuts. Set aside.

24	48	72	boneless, skinless chicken breast halves
½ pound	1 pound	1½ pounds	butter, melted

Preheat oven to 350°. Remove any visible fat and gristle from each chicken breast. Place one breast, boned side up, between 2 sheets of

Divide and Conquer

- Strategize batch sizes based on available containers/cookware.
- Chop and sauté vegetables.
- Prepare sauce.
- Prepare filling.
- Prepare and label all packaging.

plastic wrap. Working from the center to the edges, lightly pound each chicken breast with the flat side of a meat mallet to approximately ¼-inch thickness. Place approximately 1½ tablespoons filling in center of each breast. Fold in the long sides and roll up jellyroll fashion. Roll in butter and then in breadcrumb mixture. Secure with a toothpick and place seam side down on a foil-lined baking sheet. Bake until cooked through (approximately 30 to 40 minutes). Remove from oven. Cool. Place 4 breasts (or 1 per serving) in each tin. Pour sauce over chicken breasts, dividing evenly among tins. Cover with a sheet of plastic wrap, pressing down to cling to food. Apply board lid. Freeze.

Reheating Instructions

Defrost in refrigerator. Preheat oven to 350°. Remove board lid and plastic wrap. Transfer to baking dish, if desired, or bake in tin. Cover loosely with foil. Bake until heated through (approximately 30 minutes).

With any given menu, consider including an entrée with entertaining in mind. Stuffed Chicken Breasts are elegant and delicious.

Chicken with Artichoke Hearts in a Cream Sauce

Makes 6, 12, or 18 4-serving meals

(approximately 1 cup per serving)

Recommended Packaging

aluminum tins with board lids
plastic wrap

Ingredients and Instructions

6 meals 24 servings	12 meals 48 servings	18 meals 72 servings	
			olive or vegetable oil
9 pounds	18 pounds	27 pounds	boneless, skinless chicken breasts, cut into bite-sized pieces

Work in batches as necessary. In a large skillet over medium-high heat, heat oil. Add chicken to skillet and sauté, stirring occasionally, until cooked through. Transfer chicken to large bowl, removing batches from skillet with a slotted spoon. Refrigerate. Discard juices.

½ cup	1 cup	1½ cups	butter
½ cup	1 cup	1½ cups	all-purpose flour
6 cups	12 cups	18 cups	canned evaporated milk
6 cups	12 cups	18 cups	chicken stock or canned broth
4 cups	8 cups	12 cups	shredded Parmesan cheese
4 teaspoons	8 teaspoons	¼ cup	garlic, pressed or minced
4 teaspoons	8 teaspoons	¼ cup	dried basil
1 tablespoon	2 tablespoons	3 tablespoons	salt
1 teaspoon	2 teaspoons	1 tablespoon	ground black pepper
48 ounces	96 ounces	9 pounds	canned or frozen artichoke hearts, drained and chopped (may substitute broccoli florets)

Work in batches as necessary. In a large skillet over medium heat, melt butter. Stir in flour and cook 3 to 5 minutes. Slowly add evaporated milk and chicken stock or canned broth, stirring constantly until well blended. Whisk over medium heat until thickened. Add Parmesan cheese, garlic, basil, salt, and pepper, stirring until cheese is melted. Remove from heat and transfer to a large container for combining ingredients. Stir in artichoke hearts and cooked chicken. Divide evenly among tins. Cool. Cover with a sheet of plastic wrap, pressing down to cling to food. Apply board lid. Freeze.

Reheating Instructions

Defrost in refrigerator. Remove board lid and plastic wrap. Transfer to saucepan or microwave safe dish and heat thoroughly. Serve over pasta of your choice.

Chicken Breasts Chablis

Makes 6, 12, or 18 4-serving meals

(1 breast per serving)

Divide and Conquer
- Strategize batch sizes based on available containers/cookware.
- Prepare sauce.
- Prepare and label all packaging.

Recommended Packaging

aluminum tins with board lids
plastic wrap

Ingredients and Instructions

6 meals 24 servings	12 meals 48 servings	18 meals 72 servings	
1 cup	2 cups	3 cups	butter
½ cup plus 2 tablespoons	1¼ cups	1¾ cups plus 2 tablespoons	cornstarch
5 tablespoons	½ cup plus 2 tablespoons	¾ cup plus 3 tablespoons	Dijon mustard
7½ cups	15 cups	22½ cups	half and half
4 cups	8 cups	12 cups	Chablis or other white wine
1½ teaspoons	1 tablespoon	4½ teaspoons	dried tarragon
			salt and pepper

Work in batches as necessary. In a stockpot over medium heat, melt butter. Whisk in cornstarch and mustard and bring to a boil. Reduce to simmer, still whisking, and add half and half, wine, and tarragon. Whisk until thickened. Remove from heat and set aside. Season with salt and pepper.

24	48	72	
			olive or vegetable oil
			boneless, skinless chicken breast halves
1½ cups	3 cups	4½ cups	all-purpose flour
1 tablespoon	2 tablespoons	3 tablespoons	salt
1 teaspoon	2 teaspoons	1 tablespoon	ground black pepper

Preheat oven to 350°. Work in batches as necessary. In a large baking dish, thoroughly combine flour, salt, and pepper. In a large skillet over medium-high heat, heat oil. Dredge chicken in seasoned flour and sauté until lightly browned on each side. Arrange in baking dishes. Pour sauce over chicken. Cover and bake until chicken is cooked through and tender (approximately 45 minutes). Remove from oven. Place 4 breasts (or 1 per serving) in each tin. Pour sauce over chicken breasts, dividing evenly among tins. Cool. Cover with a sheet of plastic wrap, pressing down to cling to food. Apply board lid. Freeze.

Reheating Instructions

Defrost in refrigerator. Remove board lid and plastic wrap. Transfer to microwave safe dish and heat thoroughly. Alternatively, bake in container at 350° until heated through (approximately 30 minutes).

Chicken Breasts in Phyllo

Makes 6, 12, or 18 4-serving meals

(1 packet per serving)

Recommended Packaging

freezer bags
plastic wrap

Ingredients and Instructions

6 meals 24 servings	12 meals 48 servings	18 meals 72 servings	
24	**48**	**72**	**boneless, skinless chicken breast halves (individually frozen)**

Working with frozen breasts, remove any visible fat and gristle from each chicken breast. For food safety, return breasts promptly to freezer.

1½ cups	3 cups	4½ cups	**sour cream**
1½ cups	3 cups	4½ cups	**mayonnaise**
2 cups	4 cups	6 cups	**chopped green onions**
⅔ cup	1⅓ cups	2 cups	**fresh lemon juice**
2 teaspoons	4 teaspoons	2 tablespoons	**garlic, pressed or minced**
4 teaspoons	8 teaspoons	¼ cup	**dried tarragon**

In a large bowl, combine sour cream, mayonnaise, green onions, lemon juice, garlic, and tarragon. Refrigerate.

48 sheets (2½ pounds)	96 sheets (5 pounds)	144 sheets (7½ pounds)	**phyllo dough**
2½ cups	5 cups	7½ cups	**butter, melted**
1½ cups	3 cups	4½ cups	**shredded Parmesan cheese** **salt and pepper**

Defrost phyllo overnight in refrigerator. Mist a clean kitchen towel with water. Remove phyllo sheets from box; open flat and cover with towel. Remove one sheet. Brush with melted butter (approximately 2 teaspoons). Place a second sheet on top of the first and brush with melted butter. Place a breast on one end of buttered phyllo sheets. Salt and pepper breast. Spread approximately 1½ tablespoons of sauce on each side (3 tablespoons total). Sprinkle with 1 tablespoon shredded Parmesan cheese. Fold end of phyllo sheets over breast and then fold over both sides. Roll breast up in phyllo sheets to form a packet and brush with butter. Repeat with remaining breasts and phyllo sheets, keeping unused phyllo covered until ready to use, and breasts frozen until ready to use. Wrap each packet individually in plastic wrap and place 4 packets (or 1 per serving) in each freezer bag. Seal bag, pressing out excess air. Freeze immediately.

Reheating Instructions

Defrost in refrigerator. Preheat oven to 375°. Remove packaging and arrange in a baking dish, allowing space between each packet. Cover with foil to prevent excess browning. Bake until chicken is cooked through (approximately 40 minutes).

Vary recipes to suit your tastes. Chicken Breasts in Phyllo may be prepared with a variety of different fillings.

Chicken and Broccoli Quiche

Makes 6, 12, or 18 4-serving meals

(¼ quiche per serving)

Recommended Packaging

frozen pie shells in aluminum pie tins
one gallon freezer bags
foil
plastic wrap

Ingredients and Instructions

6 meals	12 meals	18 meals	
24 servings	48 servings	72 servings	
6	12	18	**boneless, skinless chicken breasts**

Bake or poach chicken. See *Preparing Chicken*. Cut into bite-sized pieces. Refrigerate. Discard juices.

6 cups	12 cups	18 cups	**broccoli, chopped into bite-sized pieces**

Steam broccoli until tender crisp. Set aside.

18	36	48	**eggs**
9 cups	18 cups	27 cups	**half and half**
¾ cup	1½ cups	2¼ cups	**lemon juice**
2 tablespoons	¼ cup	6 tablespoons	**salt**
1 teaspoon	2 teaspoons	1 tablespoon	**pepper**
6	12	18	**frozen pie shells**
6 cups	12 cups	18 cups	**shredded Swiss cheese**

Preheat oven to 375°. In a large bowl, beat together eggs, half and half, and lemon juice. Stir in salt and pepper. Divide broccoli, chicken, and cheese evenly among pie shells. Pour egg mixture over cheese, dividing evenly among tins. Bake until knife inserted in center comes out clean (approximately 30 to 40 minutes). Cool completely. Cover with plastic wrap and foil. Place in freezer bag. Seal bag, pressing out excess air. Freeze.

Reheating Instructions

Defrost in refrigerator. Preheat oven to 375°. Remove packaging. Reheat until heated through (approximately 30 minutes). Cover loosely with foil to halt browning if necessary.

Divide and Conquer
- Strategize batch sizes based on available containers/cookware.
- Cook chicken.
- Cut chicken into bite-sized pieces.
- Chop and steam broccoli.
- Prepare and label all packaging.

Purchasing frozen piecrust shells will not only save a considerable amount of time, but also provide the tin for freezing!

Chicken and Broccoli Loaf Kits

Makes 6, 12, or 18 4-serving meals

(¼ loaf per serving)

Recommended Packaging

one gallon freezer bags
one quart freezer bags
snack bags
foil
plastic wrap

Divide and Conquer

- Strategize batch sizes based on available containers/cookware.
- Cook chicken.
- Cut chicken into bite-sized pieces.
- Package frozen dough.
- Package almonds.
- Chop vegetables.
- Prepare filling.
- Package filling.
- Prepare and label all packaging.

Ingredients and Instructions

6 meals 24 servings	12 meals 48 servings	18 meals 72 servings	
6	**12**	**18**	**one pound loaves frozen bread dough**
¾ cup	**1½ cups**	**2¼ cups**	**slivered almonds (optional)**

Wrap each loaf of dough in foil or plastic wrap. Package almonds in snack bags (2 tablespoons per loaf).

6 pounds	**12 pounds**	**18 pounds**	**boneless, skinless chicken breasts**

Bake or poach chicken. See *Preparing Chicken*. Cut into bite-sized pieces. Refrigerate. Discard juices.

6 cups	**12 cups**	**18 cups**	**broccoli, chopped**
3	**6**	**9**	**red bell peppers, chopped**
2 tablespoons	**¼ cup**	**6 tablespoons**	**garlic, pressed or minced**
6 cups	**12 cups**	**18 cups**	**shredded sharp cheddar cheese**
3 cups	**6 cups**	**9 cups**	**mayonnaise**
2 tablespoons	**¼ cup**	**6 tablespoons**	**dried dill**
2 teaspoons	**4 teaspoons**	**2 tablespoons**	**salt**

Into a large bowl, place chopped broccoli, red bell pepper, garlic, cheese, mayonnaise, dill, salt, and cooked chicken, stirring until evenly combined. Divide evenly among one quart freezer bags. Seal bag, pressing out excess air. Place a loaf of frozen bread, a package of filling, and a package of almonds in each one gallon freezer bag. Include the following preparation instructions. Seal bag, pressing out excess air. Freeze.

Preparation Instructions

Remove bread from wrapping. Thaw in refrigerator (approximately 6 hours) and then set out to rise 1 to 2 hours. Or, thaw on counter (approximately 5 hours). Look for dough to double in bulk. Defrost chicken and broccoli mixture in refrigerator. Roll dough to approximately 10-inch x 14-inch. Spread chicken and vegetable mixture down center of dough. Sprinkle almonds over filling. Using a knife, cut strips in the dough on either side of the filling. Alternating side to side, pull the strips decoratively over the filling (pinch end strips to seal). Cover and allow to rise again (approximately 45 minutes). Preheat oven to 350°. Bake approximately 40 minutes. If bread browns too quickly, cover with foil to halt browning.

Alert your food exchange group to remove the bread from the freezer well in advance of serving time.

Moroccan Chicken with Apricots and Almonds

Makes 6, 12, or 18 4-serving meals

(approximately 1 cup per serving)

Recommended Packaging

aluminum tins with board lids
plastic wrap

Ingredients and Instructions

6 meals 24 servings	12 meals 48 servings	18 meals 72 servings	
			olive oil
10 pounds	**20 pounds**	**30 pounds**	**boneless, skinless chicken breasts, cut into bite sized pieces**

Work in batches as necessary. In a large skillet over medium-high heat, heat oil. Add chicken to skillet and sauté, stirring occasionally, until cooked through. Transfer chicken to large bowl, removing batches from skillet with a slotted spoon. Refrigerate. Discard juices.

3 cups	**6 cups**	**9 cups**	**whole or slivered almonds**

Package almonds in snack bags (½ cup per bag or 2 tablespoons per serving).

			olive or vegetable oil
5	**10**	**15**	**large onions, finely sliced**
5 teaspoons	**3 tablespoons plus 1 teaspoon**	**5 tablespoons**	**ground ginger**
5 teaspoons	**3 tablespoons plus 1 teaspoon**	**5 tablespoons**	**ground coriander**
2½ teaspoons	**5 teaspoons**	**7½ teaspoons**	**ground cumin**
2½ teaspoons	**5 teaspoons**	**7½ teaspoons**	**ground cinnamon**
1¼ teaspoons	**2½ teaspoons**	**3¾ teaspoons**	**ground turmeric**
2 teaspoon	**4 teaspoons**	**6 teaspoons**	**cayenne pepper**
12 cups	**24 cups**	**36 cups**	**chicken stock or canned broth**
2 pounds	**4 pounds**	**6 pounds**	**dried apricots, cut into strips**

Work in batches as necessary. In a large stockpot over medium heat, heat oil. Sauté onions until lightly browned. Add spices and sauté 2 minutes. Stir in chicken stock or canned broth and dried apricots and bring to a boil at high heat. Add cooked chicken. Reduce heat and simmer, stirring frequently, to thicken and reduce (approximately 30 minutes). Remove from heat. Divide evenly among tins. Cool. Cover with a sheet of plastic wrap, pressing down to cling to food. Place a package of almonds in each tin. Apply board lid. Freeze.

Reheating Instructions

Defrost in refrigerator. Remove board lid and plastic wrap. Transfer to saucepan or microwave safe dish and heat thoroughly. Toast almonds if desired. Serve over rice. Sprinkle with almonds.

Divide and Conquer

- Strategize batch sizes based on available containers/cookware.
- Cut chicken into bite-sized pieces.
- Cook chicken.
- Chop dried apricots.
- Chop onions.
- Prepare spice mixture.
- Package almonds.
- Prepare and label all packaging.

Chicken Cordon Bleu with Gruyere Cheese Sauce

Makes 6, 12, or 18 4-serving meals

(1 breast per serving)

Recommended Packaging   aluminum tins with board lids
plastic wrap

Ingredients and Instructions

meals	12 meals	18 meals
4 servings	48 servings	72 servings

Gruyere Cheese Sauce

			olive or vegetable oil
	1	1½	medium onions, minced
tablespoons	¾ cup	1 cup plus 2 tablespoons	butter
cup	1 cup	1½ cups	all-purpose flour
cups	10 cups	15 cups	milk
cup	2 cups	3 cups	shredded Gruyere cheese
cup	2 cups	3 cups	shredded Parmesan cheese
			salt and pepper to taste

Work in batches as necessary. In a large skillet over medium heat, heat oil. Sauté onions until tender. Remove from pan and set aside. Using the same skillet, melt butter over medium heat. Stir in flour and cook 3 to 5 minutes. Slowly add milk, stirring constantly until well blended. Whisk over medium heat until thickened. Remove from heat. Add shredded cheeses, stirring until melted. Stir in reserved onions. Season with salt and pepper. Set aside.

4	48	72	boneless, skinless chicken breast halves
4 slices	48 slices	72 slices	ham or pastrami
4 slices	48 slices	72 slices	Swiss cheese
cup	2 cups	3 cups	butter, melted

Preheat oven to 350°. Remove any visible fat and gristle from each chicken breast. Place one breast, boned side up, between 2 sheets of plastic wrap. Working from the center to the edges, lightly pound each chicken breast with the flat side of a meat mallet to approximately -inch thickness. Place a slice of ham and a slice of cheese in the middle of each breast. Fold in the long sides and roll up jellyroll fashion. Brush with butter. Bake until cooked through (approximately 30 to 40 minutes). Remove from oven. Cool. Place 4 breasts (or 1 per serving) in each tin. Pour sauce over chicken breasts, dividing evenly among tins. Cover with a sheet of plastic wrap, pressing down to cling to food. Apply board lid. Freeze.

Reheating Instructions

Defrost in refrigerator. Preheat oven to 350°. Remove board lid and plastic wrap. Transfer to baking dish, if desired, or bake in tin. Cover loosely with foil. Bake until heated through (approximately 30 minutes).

Divide and Conquer

- Strategize batch sizes based on available containers/cookware.
- Prepare sauce.
- Prepare and label all packaging.

Peruse your local restaurant-supply store and bulk warehouse. While prepared foods can be expensive, you'll often find bulk ingredients to be very favorably priced.

Divide and Conquer

- Strategize batch sizes based on available containers/cookware.
- Cook chicken.
- Cut chicken into bite-sized pieces.
- Prepare and label all packaging.

Chicken Enchilada Casserole

Makes 6, 12, or 18 4-serving meals

(approximately 1½ cups per serving)

Recommended Packaging

5"x12" or 8"x 8" (6-cup) aluminum tins
with board lids
snack bags
plastic wrap

Ingredients and Instructions

6 meals	12 meals	18 meals	
24 servings	48 servings	72 servings	
9 pounds	**18 pounds**	**27 pounds**	**boneless, skinless chicken breasts**

Bake or poach chicken. See *Preparing Chicken*. Cut into bite-sized pieces and refrigerate. Discard juices.

60 ounces	**7 lbs, 8 oz**	**11 lbs, 4 oz**	**cream of chicken soup**
2 pounds	**4 pounds**	**6 pounds**	**sour cream**
24 ounces	**48 ounces**	**72 ounces**	**mild salsa or picante sauce**
4 cups	**8 cups**	**12 cups**	**shredded Monterey Jack cheese**

In a large container, mix soup, sour cream, salsa, cheese, and cooked chicken until evenly combined. Refrigerate.

3 cups	**6 cups**	**9 cups**	**shredded cheddar cheese**

Package cheese in snack bags (½ cup per meal or 2 tablespoons per serving).

> ### Size Adjuster (9" x 13")
> Package cheese in snack bags (¾ cup per meal or 2 tablespoons per serving).

48 ounces	**96 ounces**	**9 pounds**	**mild salsa or picante sauce**
36 to 40	**72 to 80**	**108 to 120**	**6-inch soft shell corn tortillas**

Lightly spray each tin with nonstick cooking spray. Place a layer of corn tortillas across the bottom of each tin, trimmed to fit as not to overlap. Divide and spread half of filling evenly among tins. Cover with a layer of corn tortillas. Repeat. Spread 1 cup salsa (or ¼ cup per serving) over top, covering tortillas completely. Cover with a layer of plastic wrap, pressing down to cling to food. Place a package of cheese in each tin. Apply board lid. Freeze.

Size Adjuster (9" x 13")

Lightly spray each tin with nonstick cooking spray. Place a layer of corn tortillas across the bottom of each tin, trimmed to fit as not to overlap. Divide and spread half of filling evenly among tins. Cover with a layer of corn tortillas. Repeat. Spread 1½ cups salsa (or ¼ cup per serving) over top, covering tortillas completely. Cover with a layer of plastic wrap, pressing down to cling to food. Place a package of cheese in each tin. Apply board lid. Freeze.

Reheating Instructions

Defrost in refrigerator. Preheat oven to 350°. Remove board lid, cheese, and plastic wrap. Cover loosely with foil to prevent drying. Bake until bubbly around the edges and hot in the center (approximately 30 minutes). Remove foil and sprinkle with cheese during last 5 minutes of baking. Let stand at room temperature 15 minutes before cutting. Serve with black olives, sour cream, and chopped green onions, as desired.

Size Adjuster

6 Meal Equivalents	12 Meal Equivalents	18 Meal Equivalents
(6) 5" x 12" or 8" x 8"	(12) 5" x 12" or 8" x 8"	(18) 5" x 12" or 8" x 8"
(4) 9" x 13"	(8) 9" x 13"	(12) 9" x 13"

Chicken Enchiladas with Lime and Cilantro

Makes 6, 12, or 18 4-serving meals

(1 enchilada per serving)

Recommended Packaging

aluminum tins with board lids
snack bags
plastic wrap

Ingredients and Instructions

6 meals 24 servings	12 meals 48 servings	18 meals 72 servings	
9 pounds	**18 pounds**	**27 pounds**	boneless, skinless chicken breasts

Bake or poach chicken. See *Preparing Chicken*. Cut into ¼-inch cubes and refrigerate. Discard juices.

2 tablespoons	¼ cup	6 tablespoons	garlic, pressed or minced
52 ounces	6 lbs, 8 oz	9 lbs, 12 oz	mild salsa or picante sauce
6 tablespoons	¾ cup	1 cup plus 2 tablespoons	fresh lime juice
1½ cups	3 cups	4½ cups	fresh cilantro leaves
1½ cups	3 cups	4½ cups	fresh parsley
1½ cups	3 cups	4½ cups	shredded mozzarella cheese

Work in batches as necessary. Place garlic, salsa, lime juice, cilantro leaves, and fresh parsley in a blender or food processor and process until smooth. Stir all batches together before proceeding. Prepare a packet of sauce for each meal by placing sauce (1 cup per meal or ¼ cup per serving) in snack bag. Pour remaining sauce over chicken breast meat and add mozzarella cheese, stirring to combine.

6 cups	12 cups	18 cups	shredded mozzarella cheese
24	48	72	10-inch flour tortillas

Package cheese in snack bags (1 cup per bag or ¼ cup per serving). Assemble enchiladas by placing a generous ½ cup chicken mixture on each tortilla, folding ends in, and rolling. Place 4 enchiladas (or 1 per serving) in each tin. Cover with a sheet of plastic wrap, pressing down to cling to food. Place a package of sauce and a package of cheese in each tin. Apply board lid. Freeze.

Reheating Instructions

Defrost in refrigerator. Preheat oven to 350°. Remove board lid, salsa, cheese, and plastic wrap. Transfer to baking dish, if desired, or bake in tin. Spread sauce over enchiladas. Cover loosely with foil to prevent drying. Bake until bubbly around the edges and hot in the center (approximately 30 minutes). Remove foil and sprinkle with cheese during last 5 minutes of baking.

Chicken Florentine

Makes 6, 12, or 18 4-serving meals

(approximately 1 cup per serving)

Recommended Packaging   aluminum tins with board lids

plastic wrap

Ingredients and Instructions

6 meals 24 servings	12 meals 48 servings	18 meals 72 servings	
			olive or vegetable oil
10 pounds	20 pounds	30 pounds	boneless, skinless chicken breasts, cut into bite-sized pieces

Work in batches as necessary. In a large skillet over medium-high heat, heat oil. Add chicken to skillet and sauté, stirring occasionally, until cooked through. Transfer chicken to large bowl, removing batches from skillet with a slotted spoon. Refrigerate. Discard juices.

			olive or vegetable oil
3	6	9	medium onions, finely chopped
3 pounds	6 pounds	9 pounds	fresh mushrooms, sliced

Work in batches as necessary. Using the same skillet over medium heat, heat oil. Sauté onions and mushrooms until tender. Remove from pan and set aside.

1½ cups	3 cups	4½ cups	butter
2 cups	4 cups	6 cups	all-purpose flour
9 cups	18 cups	27 cups	chicken stock or canned broth
1½ pounds	3 pounds	4½ pounds	cream cheese, softened and cut into small chunks
2 pounds	4 pounds	6 pounds	fresh spinach, washed and large stems removed
			salt and pepper to taste

Work in batches as necessary. In the same skillet over medium heat, melt butter. Stir in flour and cook 3 to 5 minutes. Slowly add chicken stock or canned broth, stirring constantly until well blended. Whisk over medium heat until thickened. Stir in cream cheese chunks until melted. Remove from heat and transfer to a large container for combining ingredients. Season with salt and pepper. Stir in fresh spinach. Add cooked chicken, onions, and mushrooms. Stir until evenly combined. Divide evenly among tins. Cool. Cover with a sheet of plastic wrap, pressing down to cling to food. Apply board lid. Freeze.

Reheating Instructions

Defrost in refrigerator. Remove board lid and plastic wrap. Transfer to saucepan or microwave safe dish and gently simmer over low heat. Serve over linguini or fettuccini.

Divide and Conquer

- Strategize batch sizes based on available containers/cookware.
- Cut chicken into bite-sized pieces.
- Cook chicken.
- Chop onions.
- Clean and slice mushrooms.
- Sauté onions and mushrooms.
- Clean spinach.
- Prepare and label all packaging.

Lower the cost of preparing a recipe by reducing non-critical pricey ingredients like mushrooms, nuts, and dried fruits.

Chicken Gyro Kits

Makes 6, 12, or 18 4-serving meals

(1 gyro per serving)

Recommended Packaging

one gallon freezer bags
one quart freezer bags
snack bags
plastic wrap

Divide and Conquer

- Strategize batch sizes based on available containers/cookware.
- Cut chicken into bite-sized pieces.
- Marinate chicken.
- Cook chicken.
- Prepare Yogurt-Dill Sauce.
- Package pitas.
- Package cheese.
- Prepare and label all packaging.

Ingredients and Instructions

6 meals 24 servings	12 meals 48 servings	18 meals 72 servings	
1 cup	2 cups	3 cups	olive oil
¾ cup	1½ cups	2¼ cups	fresh lemon juice
¼ cup	½ cup	¾ cup	garlic, pressed or minced
2 tablespoons	¼ cup	6 tablespoons	dried mint
2 tablespoons	¼ cup	6 tablespoons	dried oregano
2 tablespoons	¼ cup	6 tablespoons	black pepper
1 tablespoon	2 tablespoons	3 tablespoons	salt
10 pounds	20 pounds	30 pounds	boneless, skinless chicken breasts, cut into bite sized pieces

In a medium bowl, whisk together all marinade ingredients. Pour over chicken pieces and stir to combine. Marinate, refrigerated, 2 hours. Work in batches as necessary. In a large skillet over medium-high heat, add chicken and sauté until cooked through. Transfer chicken to large bowl, removing batches from skillet with a slotted spoon. Discard juices. Cool. Divide evenly among one quart freezer bags. Seal bag, pressing out excess air. Refrigerate.

24	48	72	pitas

Wrap pitas in foil (4 per meal or 1 per serving).

12 ounces	24 ounces	36 ounces	Feta cheese, crumbled

Package cheese in snack bags (2 ounces per meal or ½ ounce per serving). Place a package of chicken, a package of pitas, and a package of cheese in each one gallon freezer bag. Seal bag, pressing out excess air. Freeze.

Yogurt-Dill Sauce

4 servings	48 servings	72 servings	
½ pounds	3 pounds	4½ pounds	cream cheese, softened
pounds	4 pounds	6 pounds	natural plain yogurt
cup	½ cup	¾ cup	fresh lemon juice
teaspoons	4 teaspoons	2 tablespoons	garlic, pressed or minced
tablespoon	2 tablespoons	3 tablespoons	dried dill
teaspoons	4 teaspoons	2 tablespoons	salt

substituting low-fat or non-fat yogurt for natural yogurt, strain overnight in refrigerator in a coffee filter-lined sieve. Combine all ingredi-
nts in a mixing bowl or processor. Beat or process until smooth. Divide evenly among tins. Cover with a sheet of plastic wrap, pressing
own to cling to food. Apply board lid. Freeze. Include one Yogurt-Dill Sauce with each Chicken Gyro Kit.

Serving Instructions

Defrost in refrigerator. Preheat oven to 350°. Warm foil-wrapped pitas in oven 10 minutes. Warm chicken in oven or microwave until
eated through. Stir yogurt-dill sauce. Transform into Tzatziki, if desired, by adding ½ large cucumber (peeled, seeded, finely diced or shred-
ed, and drained). Top pita rounds with chicken, yogurt-dill sauce, and crumbled feta. Tomatoes and onions can be added upon serving.

Express your appreciation to food exchange members by occasionally including a bonus with your entrées! Hummus, with a couple of extra pitas, would be a welcome addition to a Chicken Gyro Kit.

Chicken Lasagna with Tarragon Cheese Sauce

Makes 6, 12, or 18 4-serving meals

(approximately 1½ cups per serving)

Recommended Packaging

5"x12" or 8"x 8" (6-cup) aluminum tins
with board lids
plastic wrap

Ingredients and Instructions

6 meals	12 meals	18 meals	
24 servings	48 servings	72 servings	
10 pounds	**20 pounds**	**30 pounds**	**boneless, skinless chicken breasts**

Bake or poach chicken. See *Preparing Chicken*. Cut into bite-sized pieces and refrigerate. Discard juices.

6 tablespoons	**¾ cup**	**1 cup plus 2 tablespoons**	**butter**
3	**6**	**9**	**medium onions, chopped**
1½ pounds	**3 pounds**	**4½ pounds**	**fresh mushrooms, sliced**
6 cups	**12 cups**	**18 cups**	**chicken stock or canned broth**
2 tablespoons	**¼ cup**	**6 tablespoons**	**dried tarragon**
6 cups	**12 cups**	**18 cups**	**shredded Swiss cheese**
3 pounds	**6 pounds**	**9 pounds**	**cream cheese, softened and cut into small chunks**
			salt and pepper to taste

Work in batches as necessary. In a large stockpot over medium heat, melt butter. Sauté onions and mushrooms until tender. Stir in chicken stock or canned broth and tarragon and bring to a boil at high heat. Reduce heat and add cream cheese chunks, stirring until melted. Remove from heat. Slowly stir in shredded Swiss cheese. Season with salt and pepper. Reserve 1 cup (or ¼ cup per serving) sauce per tin in a separate container for later use in assembling lasagna. Set aside. Stir chicken into remaining sauce. Refrigerate.

Size Adjuster (9" x 13")

Reserve 1½ cups (or ⅜ cup per serving) sauce per tin in a separate container for later use in assembling lasagna. Set aside. Stir chicken into remaining sauce. Refrigerate.

3 cups	**6 cups**	**9 cups**	**shredded Swiss cheese**

Package cheese in snack bags (½ cup per meal or 2 tablespoons per serving).

Size Adjuster (9" x 13")

Package cheese in snack bags (¾ cup per meal or 2 tablespoons per serving).

| 66 | 72 | 108 | lasagna noodles, slightly undercooked |
| 6 cups | 12 cups | 18 cups | reserved cheese sauce |

Lightly spray each tin with nonstick cooking spray. Spread ½ cup (or 2 tablespoons per serving) of reserved sauce on bottom of each tin. Cover sauce with a layer of noodles. Divide and spread half of filling evenly among tins. Cover with a layer of noodles. Repeat. Spread ½ cup (or 2 tablespoons per serving) of reserved sauce over noodles. Cover with a sheet of plastic wrap, pressing down to cling to food. Place package of cheese in each tin. Apply board lid. Freeze.

Size Adjuster (9" x 13")

Lightly spray each tin with nonstick cooking spray. Spread ¾ cup (or 2 tablespoons per serving) of reserved sauce on bottom of each tin. Cover sauce with a layer of noodles. Divide and spread half of filling evenly among tins. Cover with a layer of noodles. Repeat. Spread ¾ cup (or 2 tablespoons per serving) of reserved sauce over noodles. Cover with a sheet of plastic wrap, pressing down to cling to food. Place a package of cheese in each tin. Apply board lid. Freeze.

Reheating Instructions

Defrost in refrigerator. Preheat oven to 350°. Remove board lid, cheese, and plastic wrap. Cover loosely with foil to prevent drying. Bake until bubbly around the edges and hot in the center (approximately 30 minutes). Remove foil and sprinkle with cheese during last 5 minutes of baking. Let stand 15 minutes before cutting.

Size Adjuster

6 Meal Equivalents	12 Meal Equivalents	18 Meal Equivalents
(6) 5" x 12" or 8" x 8"	(12) 5" x 12" or 8" x 8"	(18) 5" x 12" or 8" x 8"
(4) 9" x 13"	(8) 9" x 13"	(12) 9" x 13"

Chicken Parmigiana

Makes 6, 12, or 18 4-serving meals

(1 breast per serving)

Recommended Packaging

aluminum tins with board lids
snack bags
plastic wrap

Ingredients and Instructions

6 meals	12 meals	18 meals	
24 servings	48 servings	72 servings	

Tomato Sauce

2	4	6	medium onions, finely chopped
1½ teaspoons	1 tablespoon	4½ teaspoons	garlic, pressed or minced
5 tablespoons	½ cup plus 2 tablespoons	¾ cup plus 3 tablespoons	dried parsley
1½ tablespoons	3 tablespoons	4½ tablespoons	dried basil
1 tablespoon	2 tablespoons	3 tablespoons	dried oregano
6	12	18	bay leaves
1 teaspoon	2 teaspoons	1 tablespoon	ground black pepper
72 ounces	9 pounds	13 lbs, 8 oz	canned tomato sauce
24 ounces	48 ounces	72 ounces	canned chopped tomatoes, undrained

Place all the ingredients in a large stockpot. Cover and bring to a boil. Uncover, reduce heat, and simmer, stirring occasionally, for 1 hour. Remove from heat and set aside. Remove and discard bay leaves.

6 cups	12 cups	18 cups	shredded mozzarella cheese

Package cheese in snack bags (1 cup per meal or ¼ cup per serving). Refrigerate.

2 cups	4 cups	6 cups	grated Parmesan cheese
10 ounces	20 ounces	30 ounces	plain breadcrumbs
2 teaspoons	4 teaspoons	2 tablespoons	garlic powder
2 teaspoons	4 teaspoons	2 tablespoons	salt or seasoned salt

Place all ingredients in a bowl. Stir to combine. Set aside.

24	48	72	boneless, skinless chicken breast halves
1 cup	2 cups	3 cups	butter, melted

Preheat oven to 350°. Remove any visible fat and gristle from each chicken breast. Work in batches as necessary. Dip rinsed breast in melted butter and dredge in breadcrumb coating. Lay breasts flat on 2 foil-lined baking trays. Place trays in oven. Bake 25 minutes; switch

---

Divide and Conquer

- ☞ Strategize batch sizes based on available containers/cookware.
- ☞ Prepare sauce.
- ☞ Package cheese.
- ☞ Prepare breading.
- ☞ Prepare and label all packaging.

etween oven racks and bake 25 minutes longer. Meanwhile, pour sauce (1 cup per meal or ¼ cup per serving) in bottom of each tin.
emove breasts from oven. Cool. Place 4 breasts (or 1 per serving) in each tin. Cover with sauce (1 cup per meal or ¼ cup per serving).
over with a sheet of plastic wrap, pressing down to cling to food. Place a package of cheese in each tin. Apply board lid. Freeze.

Reheating Instructions

efrost in refrigerator. Preheat oven to 350°. Remove board lid, cheese, and plastic wrap. Transfer to baking dish, if desired, or bake in tin.
over loosely with foil to prevent drying. Bake until bubbly around the edges and hot in center (approximately 30 minutes). Remove foil
nd sprinkle with cheese during last 5 minutes of baking.

Freeze fresh herbs when in season. Carefully wash and dry. Place whole or chopped leaves and/or stems in muffin cups. Top with cold water, submerging pieces. Freeze until solid. When ready to use, place the cubes in a strainer under cold running water until defrosted. Use immediately.

Chicken with Sun Dried Tomatoes in a Cream Sauce

Makes 6, 12, or 18 4-serving meals

(approximately 1 cup per serving)

Divide and Conquer

- Strategize batch sizes based on available containers/cookware.
- Prepare dredging mixture.
- Cut chicken into bite-sized pieces.
- Cook chicken.
- Chop sun dried tomatoes.
- Prepare and label all packaging.

Consider drying your own tomatoes! Your group may wish to purchase a shared food dehydrator and put it to work during the summer months when tomatoes are most plentiful and most delicious. Consider dehydrating fruits and mushrooms as well.

Recommended Packaging

aluminum tins with board lids
plastic wrap

Ingredients and Instructions

6 meals 24 servings	12 meals 48 servings	18 meals 72 servings	
			olive or vegetable oil
9 pounds	18 pounds	27 pounds	boneless, skinless chicken breasts, cut into bite sized pieces
1½ cups	3 cups	4½ cups	all-purpose flour
1 tablespoon	2 tablespoons	3 tablespoons	salt
1 teaspoon	2 teaspoons	1 tablespoon	ground black pepper

Work in batches as necessary. In a large baking dish, thoroughly combine flour, salt, and pepper. In a large skillet over medium-high, heat oil. Dredge chicken in seasoned flour and sauté until cooked through. Using tongs, transfer chicken to large bowl. Refrigerate.

6 tablespoons	¾ cup	1 cup plus 2 tablespoons	butter
6 tablespoons	¾ cup	1 cup plus 2 tablespoons	all-purpose flour
6 cups	12 cups	18 cups	chicken stock or canned broth
6 cups	12 cups	18 cups	heavy cream
1½ cups	3 cups	4½ cups	canned evaporated milk
1½ cups	3 cups	4½ cups	dry white wine
3 tablespoons	6 tablespoons	9 tablespoons	Dijon mustard
1 tablespoon	2 tablespoons	3 tablespoons	dried basil
1½ cups	3 cups	4½ cups	sun dried tomatoes, chopped into small pieces
			salt and pepper to taste

Work in batches as necessary. In a large skillet over medium heat, melt butter. Stir in flour and cook 3 to 5 minutes. Slowly add chicken stock or canned broth, cream, evaporated milk, and wine, stirring constantly until well blended. Whisk over medium heat until thickened. Stir in Dijon mustard and basil. Remove from heat and transfer to a large container for combining ingredients. Stir in sun dried tomatoes and cooked chicken. Season with salt and pepper. Divide evenly among tins. Cool. Cover with a sheet of plastic wrap, pressing down to cling to food. Apply board lid. Freeze.

Reheating Instructions

Defrost in refrigerator. Remove board lid and plastic wrap. Transfer to saucepan or microwave safe dish and heat thoroughly. Serve with pasta of your choice.

Greek Chicken

Makes 6, 12, or 18 4-serving meals

(approximately 1 cup per serving)

Recommended Packaging   aluminum tins with board lids
plastic wrap

Ingredients and Instructions

meals 4 servings	12 meals 48 servings	18 meals 72 servings	
			olive or vegetable oil
pounds	18 pounds	27 pounds	boneless, skinless chicken breasts, cut into large pieces
½ cups	3 cups	4½ cups	all-purpose flour
tablespoon	2 tablespoons	3 tablespoons	salt
teaspoon	2 teaspoons	1 tablespoon	ground black pepper

Work in batches as necessary. In a large baking dish, thoroughly combine flour, salt, and pepper. In a large skillet over medium-high heat, heat oil. Dredge chicken in seasoned flour and sauté until cooked through. Using tongs, transfer chicken to large bowl. Refrigerate.

			olive or vegetable oil
pounds	4 pounds	6 pounds	fresh mushrooms, sliced
tablespoons	¼ cup	6 tablespoons	garlic, pressed or minced
cups	18 cups	27 cups	chicken stock or canned broth
½ cups	3 cups	4½ cups	fresh lemon juice
½ cups	3 cups	4½ cups	dry white wine
tablespoons	¼ cup	6 tablespoons	dried oregano

Work in batches as necessary. In a large stockpot, heat oil over medium-high heat. Sauté mushrooms and garlic until mushrooms brown (increase heat if necessary to evaporate liquid). Stir in chicken stock or canned broth, lemon juice, wine, and oregano and simmer until sauce is slightly reduced (approximately 30 minutes). Stir in cooked chicken and simmer 5 to 10 minutes, stirring frequently. Divide evenly among tins. Cool. Cover with a sheet of plastic wrap, pressing down to cling to food. Apply board lid. Freeze.

Reheating Instructions

Defrost in refrigerator. Remove board lid and plastic wrap. Transfer to saucepan or microwave safe dish and heat thoroughly. Serve with rice or pasta. Top with Kalamata olives and feta cheese, as desired.

Divide and Conquer

- Strategize batch sizes based on available containers/cookware.
- Prepare dredging mixture.
- Cut chicken into large pieces.
- Cook chicken.
- Clean and slice mushrooms.
- Prepare and label all packaging.

Use a food processor to chop onions, carrots, celery, cheese, mushrooms, bread, or cracker crumbs. With this kind of volume, it's finally worth getting it dirty!

Chicken and Vegetable Lasagna with a White Sauce

Makes 6, 12, or 18 4-serving meals
(approximately 1½ cups per meal)

Recommended Packaging

5" x 12" or 8" x 8" (6-cup) aluminum tins
with board lids
snack bags
plastic wrap

Ingredients and Instructions

6 meals 24 servings	12 meals 48 servings	18 meals 72 servings	
3 pounds	**6 pounds**	**9 pounds**	**boneless, skinless chicken breasts**

Bake or poach chicken. See *Preparing Chicken*. Cut into bite-sized pieces and refrigerate. Discard juices.

1½ cups	**3 cups**	**4½ cups**	**butter**
3	**6**	**9**	**medium onions, finely chopped**
2 teaspoons	**4 teaspoons**	**2 tablespoons**	**garlic, pressed or minced**
1½ cups	**3 cups**	**4½ cups**	**all-purpose flour**
6 cups	**12 cups**	**18 cups**	**chicken stock or canned broth**
6 cups	**12 cups**	**18 cups**	**milk**
6 cups	**12 cups**	**18 cups**	**shredded mozzarella cheese**
1½ cups	**3 cups**	**4½ cups**	**shredded Parmesan cheese**
5 teaspoons	**10 teaspoons**	**5 tablespoons**	**dried basil**
1 tablespoon	**2 tablespoons**	**3 tablespoons**	**dried oregano**
1 tablespoon	**2 tablespoon**	**3 tablespoons**	**salt**
2 teaspoons	**4 teaspoons**	**2 tablespoons**	**ground black pepper**

Work in batches as necessary. In a large stockpot over medium heat, melt butter. Sauté onion and garlic until tender. Stir in flour and cook 3 to 5 minutes. Slowly add chicken stock or canned broth and milk, stirring constantly until well blended. Whisk over medium heat until thickened. Remove from heat. Slowly stir in cheeses until melted. Stir in basil, oregano, salt, and pepper. Set aside.

6 cups	**12 cups**	**18 cups**	**vegetables of choice**

Chop or dice vegetables into small pieces. In a large stockpot, blanch or lightly steam summer squash, zucchini, carrots, asparagus, cauliflower, or broccoli. Thoroughly drain frozen spinach, and squeeze to remove excess liquid. Fresh spinach may be washed, dried, and layered in the lasagna.

1½ cups	**3 cups**	**4½ cups**	**shredded Parmesan cheese**

Package cheese in snack bags (¼ cup per meal or 1 tablespoon per serving).

Divide and Conquer
- ✎ Strategize batch sizes based on available containers/cookware.
- ✎ Cook chicken.
- ✎ Cut chicken into bite-sized pieces.
- ✎ Chop vegetables.
- ✎ Cook vegetables.
- ✎ Package cheese.
- ✎ Prepare and label all packaging.

Size Adjuster (9" x 13")

Package cheese in snack bags (6 tablespoons per meal or 1 tablespoon per serving).

	72	108	lasagna noodles, slightly undercooked
ξ pounds	**3 pounds**	**4½ pounds**	**ricotta cheese**
cups	**12 cups**	**18 cups**	**shredded mozzarella cheese**

ghtly spray each tin with nonstick cooking spray. Spread ½ cup (or 2 tablespoons per serving) of sauce on bottom of each tin. Cover ice with a layer of noodles. Divide and spread half of ricotta cheese evenly among tins. Divide and spread half of mozzarella cheese evenly nong tins. Divide and spread half of chicken evenly among tins. Divide and spread half of vegetable mixture evenly among tins. Cover th 1 cup (or ¼ cup per serving) sauce. Repeat. Top with a final layer of noodles and ½ cup (or 2 tablespoons per serving) sauce. Cover th a sheet of plastic wrap, pressing down to cling to food. Place a package of cheese in each tin. Apply board lid. Freeze.

Size Adjuster (9" x 13")

Lightly spray each tin with nonstick cooking spray. Spread ¾ cup (or 2 tablespoons per serving) of sauce on bottom of each tin. Cover sauce with a layer of noodles. Divide and spread half of ricotta cheese evenly among tins. Divide and spread half of mozzarella cheese evenly among tins. Divide and spread half of chicken evenly among tins. Divide and spread half of vegetable mixture evenly among tins. Cover with 1½ cups (or ¼ cup per serving) sauce. Repeat. Top with a final layer of noodles and ¾ cup (or 2 tablespoons per serving) sauce. Cover with a sheet of plastic wrap, pressing down to cling to food. Place a package of cheese in each tin. Apply board lid. Freeze.

eheating Instructions

efrost in refrigerator. Preheat oven to 350°. Remove board lid, cheese, and plastic wrap. Cover loosely with foil to prevent drying. Bake itil bubbly around the edges and hot in center (approximately 30 to 40 minutes). Remove foil and sprinkle with Parmesan cheese during st 5 minutes of baking. Let stand 15 minutes before cutting.

Size Adjuster

6 Meal Equivalents	12 Meal Equivalents	18 Meal Equivalents
(6) 5" x 12" or 8" x 8"	(12) 5" x 12" or 8" x 8"	(18) 5" x 12" or 8" x 8"
(4) 9" x 13"	(8) 9" x 13"	(12) 9" x 13"

Coq Au Vin (Chicken in Wine)

Makes 6, 12, or 18 4-serving meals

(approximately 1 cup per serving)

Recommended Packaging

aluminum tins with board lids
plastic wrap

Ingredients and Instructions

6 meals 24 servings	12 meals 48 servings	18 meals 72 servings	
			olive or vegetable oil
10 pounds	20 pounds	30 pounds	boneless, skinless chicken breasts, cut into bite-sized pieces

Work in batches as necessary. In a large skillet over medium-high heat, heat oil. Add chicken to skillet and sauté, stirring occasionally, until cooked through. Transfer chicken to large bowl, removing batches from skillet with a slotted spoon. Refrigerate. Discard juices.

6 meals	12 meals	18 meals	
1½ pounds	3 pounds	4½ pounds	bacon

In the same skillet over medium heat (or in oven), cook bacon until crisp. Drain and crumble or chop bacon. Refrigerate.

6 meals	12 meals	18 meals	
			olive or vegetable oil
1½ pounds	3 pounds	4½ pounds	carrots, cut into 1-inch lengths
1½ pounds	3 pounds	4½ pounds	pearl onions (fresh or frozen)
12 ounces	24 ounces	36 ounces	fresh mushrooms, sliced
2 tablespoons	¼ cup	6 tablespoons	garlic, pressed or minced
¼ cup	½ cup	¾ cup	butter
½ cup	1 cup	1½ cups	cornstarch
5 cups	10 cups	15 cups	chicken stock or canned broth
5 cups	10 cups	15 cups	dry red wine (Burgundy or Cabernet)
4 ounces	8 ounces	12 ounces	tomato paste
2 tablespoons	¼ cup	6 tablespoons	red currant jelly
2 tablespoons	¼ cup	6 tablespoons	brown sugar, packed
2 teaspoons	4 teaspoons	2 tablespoons	dried thyme
2	4	6	bay leaves
			salt and pepper to taste

Work in batches as necessary. In a large skillet over medium-high heat, heat oil. Sauté carrots and onions until just beginning to brown. Stir in garlic and cook 5 minutes longer. Add butter and mushrooms and cook 5 more minutes. Sprinkle with cornstarch and cook, stirring, 3 minutes longer. Add chicken stock or canned broth and wine. Bring to a boil and cook, scraping the bottom occasionally to loosen browned bits, until sauce thickens slightly. Stir in tomato paste, red currant jelly, brown sugar, thyme, and bay leaves. Gently stir in sautéed chicken and cooked bacon. Season with salt and pepper. Reduce heat and simmer uncovered 30 minutes, stirring occasionally. Cover and simmer 30 more minutes or until carrots are tender. Or, remove to baking dishes and bake 30 minutes, uncovered, at 350°. Cover and

Divide and Conquer

- ☺ Strategize batch sizes based on available containers/cookware.
- ☺ Cook and chop bacon.
- ☺ Cut chicken into bite-sized pieces.
- ☺ Cook chicken.
- ☺ Chop and sauté carrots and onions.
- ☺ Clean and slice mushrooms.
- ☺ Prepare and label all packaging.

ontinue baking another 30 minutes or until carrots are tender. Remove and discard bay leaves. Divide evenly among tins. Cool. Cover ith a sheet of plastic wrap, pressing down to cling to food. Apply board lid. Freeze.

Reheating Instructions

Defrost in refrigerator. Remove board lid and plastic wrap. Transfer to saucepan or microwave safe dish and heat thoroughly. Serve over ce, noodles, or mashed potatoes.

Cleaned and cut baby carrots are an attractive labor-saving substitution for whole carrots!

Creamed Chicken with Dill and Savory Biscuit Mix

Makes 6, 12, or 18 4-serving meals
(approximately 1 cup per serving)

Recommended Packaging

aluminum tins with board lids
freezer bags
plastic wrap

Divide and Conquer

- Strategize batch sizes based on available containers/cookware.
- Prepare biscuit mix.
- Cook chicken.
- Cut chicken into bite-sized pieces.
- Cube ham.
- Clean and slice mushrooms.
- Sauté mushrooms.
- Dice carrots.
- Mince shallots.
- Sauté carrots and shallots.
- Prepare and label all packaging.

Ingredients and Instructions

6 meals	12 meals	18 meals	
24 servings	48 servings	72 servings	
6 pounds	**12 pounds**	**18 pounds**	**boneless, skinless chicken breasts**

Bake or poach chicken. See *Preparing Chicken*. Cut into bite-sized pieces and refrigerate. Discard juices.

¾ pound	**1½ pounds**	**2¼ pounds**	**cooked ham**

Chop or dice ham in small pieces. Refrigerate.

3 tablespoons	**6 tablespoons**	**9 tablespoons**	**butter**
12 ounces	**1½ pounds**	**2¼ pounds**	**fresh mushrooms, sliced**
2 tablespoons	**¼ cup**	**6 tablespoons**	**shallots, minced**
1½ pounds	**3 pounds**	**4½ pounds**	**carrots, finely diced**

Work in batches as necessary. In a large skillet over medium heat, melt butter. Sauté mushrooms until tender (increase heat if necessary to evaporate liquid). Remove from pan and set aside. In the same skillet, melt butter and sauté carrots and shallots until tender. Remove from pan and add to sautéed mushrooms. Set aside.

¾ cup	**1½ cups**	**2¼ cups**	**butter**
¾ cup	**1½ cups**	**2¼ cups**	**all-purpose flour**
7 cups	**14 cups**	**21 cups**	**chicken stock or canned broth**
4 cups	**8 cups**	**12 cups**	**heavy cream**
¼ cup	**½ cup**	**¾ cup**	**lemon juice**
2 tablespoons	**¼ cup**	**6 tablespoons**	**dried dill**
16 ounces	**32 ounches**	**48 ounces**	**frozen peas**
			salt and pepper to taste

Work in batches as necessary. In the same skillet over medium heat, melt butter. Stir in flour and cook 3 to 5 minutes. Slowly add chicken stock or canned broth and cream, stirring constantly until well blended. Whisk over medium heat until thickened. Add lemon juice, dill, frozen peas, sautéed vegetables, cooked chicken, and cubed ham, stirring until evenly combined. Season with salt and pepper. Divide evenly among tins. Cool. Cover with a sheet of plastic wrap, pressing down to cling to food. Apply board lid. Freeze.

Reheating Instructions

Defrost in refrigerator. Remove board lid and plastic wrap. Transfer to saucepan or microwave safe dish and heat thoroughly. Serve over biscuits.

Savory Biscuit Mix

Makes 24, 48, or 72 biscuits

As an alternative to preparing a biscuit mix, supply group members with refrigerated or frozen biscuits.

24 biscuits	48 biscuits	72 biscuits	
cups	12 cups	18 cups	all-purpose flour
tablespoons	6 tablespoons	½ cup plus 1 tablespoon	baking powder
tablespoons	¼ cup	6 tablespoons	dried chives
tablespoon	2 tablespoons	3 tablespoons	dried dill
tablespoon	2 tablespoons	3 tablespoons	sugar
½ teaspoons	1 tablespoon	4½ teaspoons	salt
½ teaspoons	1 tablespoon	4½ teaspoons	ground black pepper
teaspoon	1½ teaspoons	2¼ teaspoons	paprika
cup plus 2 ablespoons	2¼ cups	3¼ cups plus 6 tablespoons	butter, chilled

Work in batches of no more than 24 biscuits. In a large bowl or processor, stir together all dry ingredients. Cut in butter using a pastry knife, fork, or processor. For each 4 biscuit serving, package and freeze 1⅓ cups dry mix in a freezer bag. Seal bag, pressing out excess air. Freeze.

Baking Instructions

Preheat oven to 450º. Bring mix to room temperature and place in bowl. For each 4 biscuit serving, add 6 tablespoons half and half. Stir gently until mixture forms a ball. On a lightly floured surface, pat into a square, approximately ¾-inch thick. Cut into squares. Place on a baking sheet and bake until golden (approximately 15 minutes).

Curried Chicken

Makes 6, 12, or 18 4-serving meals

(approximately 1 cup per serving)

Recommended Packaging

aluminum tins with board lids
plastic wrap

Ingredients and Instructions

Divide and Conquer

- Strategize batch sizes based on available containers/cookware.
- Cut chicken into bite-sized pieces.
- Chop onions.
- Peel and mince ginger.
- Prepare spice mixture.
- Prepare and label all packaging.

6 meals 24 servings	12 meals 48 servings	18 meals 72 servings	
			olive or vegetable oil
4	8	12	medium onions, chopped
6 tablespoons	¾ cup	1 cup plus 2 tablespoons	fresh ginger, minced
2½ teaspoons	5 teaspoons	7½ teaspoons	garlic, pressed or minced
5 tablespoons	½ cup plus 2 tablespoons	¾ cup plus 3 tablespoons	curry powder
1½ teaspoons	1 tablespoon	4½ teaspoons	ground cumin
½ teaspoon	1 teaspoon	1½ teaspoons	ground cinnamon
3 tablespoons	6 tablespoons	9 tablespoons	all-purpose flour
1½ cups	3 cups	4½ cups	plain yogurt
3 ounces	6 ounces	9 ounces	tomato paste
4½ cups	9 cups	13½ cups	chicken stock or canned broth
1½ cups	3 cups	4½ cups	unsweetened applesauce

Work in batches as necessary. In a large skillet over medium heat, heat oil. Sauté onions until golden. Add ginger and garlic and sauté for 2 minutes. Add curry, cumin, and cinnamon and sauté for 1 minute. Stir in flour. Add yogurt and tomato paste, whisking until sauce is smooth. Add chicken stock or canned broth and applesauce and bring to a boil. Reduce heat and simmer 30 minutes. Sauce will slightly thicken.

8 pounds	16 pounds	24 pounds	boneless, skinless chicken breasts, cut into bite-sized pieces
½ pound	1 pound	1½ pounds	sour cream
¾ cup	1½ cups	2¼ cups	canned unsweetened coconut milk
16 ounces	32 ounces	48 ounces	frozen peas salt and pepper to taste

Add chicken to sauce, simmering until chicken is almost cooked through. Stir in sour cream and coconut milk. Reduce heat to medium-low and simmer, stirring occasionally, until chicken is cooked through and sauce thickens enough to coat spoon (do not boil). Season with salt and pepper. Stir in frozen peas. Divide evenly among tins. Cool. Cover with a sheet of plastic wrap, pressing down to cling to food. Apply board lid. Freeze.

Reheating Instructions

Defrost in refrigerator. Remove board lid and plastic wrap. Transfer to saucepan or microwave safe dish and heat thoroughly. Add cayenne pepper to taste. Serve over rice. Condiment accompaniments may include mango chutney, sliced peeled bananas, chopped pitted mangoes, shredded unsweetened coconut, and chopped toasted peanuts.

Have a new recipe to try on the group? Consider preparing it for a taste test at an exchange gathering!

Hunan Chicken

Makes 6, 12, or 18 4-serving meals

(approximately 1 cup per serving)

| Recommended Packaging | aluminum tins with board lids |
| | plastic wrap |

Ingredients and Instructions

| 6 meals | 12 meals | 18 meals |
| 24 servings | 48 servings | 72 servings |

Shopping List

6 meals	12 meals	18 meals	
12 pounds	**24 pounds**	**36 pounds**	boneless, skinless chicken breasts, cut into bite-sized pieces
2¼ cups	**4½ cups**	**6¾ cups**	soy sauce
¾ cup	**1½ cups**	**2¼ cups**	cornstarch
2¼ cups	**4½ cups**	**6¾ cups**	water
1 cup plus 2 tablespoons	**2¼ cups**	**3¼ cups plus 6 tablespoons**	rice vinegar
¾ cup	**1½ cups**	**2¼ cups**	sugar
¾ cup	**1½ cups**	**2¼ cups**	sesame oil
3 bunches	**6 bunches**	**9 bunches**	green onions, chopped into 1-inch pieces
¾ cup	**1½ cups**	**2¼ cups**	chili-garlic sauce
7 tablespoons	**¾ cup plus 2 tablespoons**	**1¼ cups plus 1 tablespoon**	garlic, pressed or minced
¾ cup	**1½ cups**	**2¼ cups**	fresh ginger, minced
6 cups	**12 cups**	**18 cups**	broccoli florets
¾ cup	**1½ cups**	**2¼ cups**	peanut oil

Instructions

6 cups	**12 cups**	**18 cups**	broccoli florets

Steam broccoli until tender crisp. Divide evenly among tins (approximately 1 cup per meal or ¼ cup per serving).

Prepare 3 batches of the following:	Prepare 6 batches of the following:	Prepare 9 batches of the following:	
4 pounds			boneless, skinless chicken breasts, cut into bite-sized pieces
¼ cup			soy sauce
2 tablespoons			cornstarch

Stir together chicken, soy sauce, and cornstarch (each batch in a separate container). Refrigerate.

Divide and Conquer

- Cut chicken into bite-sized pieces.
- Clean and chop broccoli.
- Steam broccoli.
- Clean and chop green onions.
- Peel and mince ginger.
- Assemble sauce batches.
- Prepare and label all packaging.

bunch	**green onions, chopped into 1-inch pieces**
cup	**chili-garlic sauce**
½ tablespoons	**garlic, pressed or minced**
cup	**fresh ginger, minced**

ortion together green onion, chili-garlic sauce, garlic, and ginger (each batch in a separate container). Set aside.

cup	**soy sauce**
tablespoons	**cornstarch**
cup	**water**
tablespoons	**rice vinegar**
cup	**sugar**
cup	**sesame oil**

tir together soy sauce, cornstarch, water, rice vinegar, sugar, and sesame oil (each batch in a separate container). Set aside.

cup	**peanut oil**

Heat peanut oil in wok or large non-stick skillet over high heat until very hot. Add one batch chicken mixture and stir-fry 4 minutes. Using slotted spoon, transfer chicken to medium bowl. Add one batch green onion mixture and stir-fry 3 minutes. Return chicken and add one batch soy sauce mixture. Cook until chicken is cooked through and sauce thickens, about 4 minutes. Divide evenly among tins (approximately 3 cups per meal or ¾ cup per serving), pouring over broccoli. Repeat with remaining batches. Cool. Cover each tin with a sheet of plastic wrap, pressing down to cling to food. Apply board lid. Freeze.

Reheating Instructions

Defrost in refrigerator. Remove board lid and plastic wrap. Transfer to saucepan or microwave safe dish and reheat thoroughly. Serve with rice.

Check neighborhood ethnic stores as a great source for imported ingredients at knock-your-socks-off pricing!

White Chicken Chili

Makes 6, 12, or 18 4-serving meals

(approximately 1½ cups per serving)

Recommended Packaging — freezer bags or aluminum tins with board lids
plastic wrap

Ingredients and Instructions

6 meals 24 servings	12 meals 48 servings	18 meals 72 servings	
2½ pounds **9 pounds**	**5 pounds** **18 pounds**	**7½ pounds** **27 pounds**	**dry great northern white beans or** **canned white beans, drained and rinsed**

In a large stockpot cover beans with water and soak overnight. Drain and rinse. Return to stockpot, cover with water and simmer 1 hour or until desired tenderness. Drain and set aside.

6 cups **2 cups**	**12 cups** **4 cups**	**18 cups** **6 cups**	**cooked beans (from above beans)** **chicken stock or canned broth**

Work in batches as necessary. Purée half of beans with chicken stock or canned broth in a blender or food processor. Set aside. Reserve other half to return to chili.

9 pounds	**18 pounds**	**27 pounds**	**boneless, skinless chicken breasts**

Bake or poach chicken. See *Preparing Chicken*. Cut into bite-sized pieces and refrigerate. Discard juices.

			olive or vegetable oil
3	**6**	**9**	**medium onions, chopped**
1	**2**	**3**	**yellow or red bell pepper, seeded and diced** **(may substitute green bell pepper)**
1 tablespoon	**2 tablespoons**	**3 tablespoons**	**garlic, pressed or minced**

Work in batches as necessary. In a large skillet or Dutch oven over medium heat, heat oil. Sauté onions, peppers, and garlic until tender. Remove from heat and set aside.

1 cup	**2 cups**	**3 cups**	**butter**
1 cup	**2 cups**	**3 cups**	**all-purpose flour**
8 cups	**16 cups**	**24 cups**	**chicken stock or canned broth**
3 cups	**6 cups**	**9 cups**	**half and half**
3 tablespoons	**6 tablespoons**	**9 tablespoons**	**chili powder**
3 tablespoons	**6 tablespoons**	**9 tablespoons**	**ground cumin**
3 tablespoons	**6 tablespoons**	**9 tablespoons**	**Tabasco sauce**
16 ounces	**32 ounces**	**48 ounces**	**canned chopped mild green chilies**
5 cups	**10 cups**	**15 cups**	**shredded Monterey Jack cheese**
1½ pounds	**3 pounds**	**4½ pounds**	**sour cream**

Divide and Conquer

- Strategize batch sizes based on available containers/cookware.
- Cook chicken.
- Cut chicken into bite-sized pieces.
- Soak beans.
- Cook beans.
- Purée beans.
- Chop and sauté vegetables.
- Prepare and label all packaging.

Work in batches as necessary. In a large stockpot over medium heat, melt butter. Stir in flour and cook 3 to 5 minutes. Slowly add chicken stock or canned broth and half and half, stirring constantly until well blended. Whisk over medium heat until thickened. Stir in sautéed vegetables, chili powder, cumin, Tabasco sauce, and green chilies. Add puréed bean mixture and simmer 5 to 10 minutes. Remove from heat and transfer to a large container for combining ingredients. Stir in shredded cheese and sour cream. Add remaining beans and cooked chicken and stir until evenly combined. Cool. Divide evenly among freezer bags. Seal bag, pressing out excess air. Freeze.

Reheating Instructions

Defrost in refrigerator. Transfer to saucepan or microwave safe dish and heat thoroughly. Serve with a dollop of sour cream, chopped fresh tomato, and grated cheese, if desired.

Looking for a jumbo container for combining ingredients? Consider a storage bin. Store packaging materials between cooking sessions and, after a thorough washing, put it to work as one very big bowl!

Turkey

Preparing Turkey

Roasting Turkey

Turkey(s)
Water
Salt
For each 15 pounds of turkey:
3 large celery ribs, cut into 2-inch pieces
1 large onion, quartered
1 large carrot, cut into 2-inch pieces

Sprinkle cavity of turkey generously with salt and pepper. Arrange a bed of celery, onion, and carrot pieces in a large roasting pan. Place turkey on vegetables and arrange neck and gizzard (if available) alongside. Salt top of turkey. Add approximately three inches of water to bottom of pan. If desired, insert oven-safe meat thermometer into thickest part of thigh for whole turkeys or into thickest part of breast for turkey breasts. Cover and roast at 325° (see *Roasting Schedule* below). Reserve stock.

Roasting Schedule, Whole Turkeys

Net Weight Unstuffed Turkey

10 to 18 pounds 3 to 3½ hours
18 to 22 pounds 3½ to 4 hours
22 to 24 pounds 4 to 4½ hours
24 to 30 pounds 4½ to 5 hours

Turkey is done when meat thermometer reaches 180° to 185° deep in thigh. Juices should be clear, not pink, when thigh muscle is deeply pierced.

Roasting Schedule, Bone-In Turkey Breasts

Net Weight

4 to 6 pounds 1¾ to 2½ hours
6 to 8 pounds 2½ to 3¼ hours
8 to 10 pounds 3 to 3½ hours
10 to 12 pounds 3½ to 4 hours
12 to 14 pounds 4 to 4¾ hours

Turkey is done when meat thermometer reaches 180° to 185° in thickest part of the breast, just above rib bones. Juices should be clear, not pink, when breast is deeply pierced.

Turkey Tetrazzini

Makes 6, 12, or 18 4-serving meals
(approximately 1 cup per serving)

Recommended Packaging

aluminum tins with board lids
plastic wrap

Ingredients and Instructions

| 6 meals | 12 meals | 18 meals | |
24 servings	48 servings	72 servings	
2	4	6	6 to 7 pound turkey breasts

Cook turkey breast. See *Preparing Turkey.* Cool. Debone and cut turkey into chunks. Refrigerate. Reserve stock and reduce to taste.

1 cup	2 cups	3 cups	butter
1 cup	2 cups	3 cups	all-purpose flour
8 cups	16 cups	24 cups	turkey stock or canned chicken broth (include reserved stock)
6 cups	12 cups	18 cups	canned evaporated milk
6 cups	12 cups	18 cups	shredded Parmesan cheese
1 tablespoon	2 tablespoons	3 tablespoons	nutmeg
16 ounces	32 ounces	48 ounces	frozen peas
			salt and pepper to taste

Work in batches as necessary. In a large skillet over medium heat, melt butter. Stir in flour and cook 3 to 5 minutes. Slowly add turkey stock or canned broth and evaporated milk, stirring constantly until well blended. Whisk over medium heat until thickened. Add Parmesan cheese and nutmeg, stirring until cheese is melted. Remove from heat and transfer to a large container for combining ingredients. Season with salt and pepper. Stir in turkey chunks and peas. Divide evenly among tins. Cover with a sheet of plastic wrap, pressing down to cling to food. Apply board lid. Freeze.

Reheating Instructions

Defrost in refrigerator. Remove board lid and plastic wrap. Transfer to saucepan or microwave safe dish and heat thoroughly. Prepare spaghetti. Mix spaghetti and sauce together before serving.

Divide and Conquer
- ✐ Strategize batch sizes based on available containers/cookware.
- ✐ Roast turkey.
- ✐ Cut turkey into chunks.
- ✐ Prepare and label all packaging.

Pasta toppers can be prepared inclusive or exclusive of pasta, based on your group's preference. When included, substantially undercook pasta for al dente reheating.

Roasted Turkey with Dried Cranberries and Herbed Stuffing

Makes 6, 12, or 18 4-serving meals

(approximately 1 cup per serving)

Recommended Packaging

aluminum tins with board lids
plastic wrap

Ingredients and Instructions

6 meals 24 servings	12 meals 48 servings	18 meals 72 servings	
2	**4**	**6**	**6 to 7 pound turkey breasts**

Roast turkey breasts. See *Preparing Turkey*. Cool. Debone and cut turkey into large chunks. Refrigerate. Reserve stock and reduce to taste.

12 ounces	**24 ounces**	**36 ounces**	**dried cranberries**
2 cups	**4 cups**	**6 cups**	**port wine**

Combine cranberries and port wine in a microwave safe bowl. Microwave on high for 2 minutes or until hot. Set aside.

¾ cup	**1½ cups**	**2¼ cups**	**butter**
3	**6**	**9**	**medium onions, chopped**
1 tablespoon	**2 tablespoons**	**3 tablespoons**	**dried thyme**
1½ cups	**3 cups**	**4½ cups**	**all-purpose flour**
12 cups	**24 cups**	**36 cups**	**turkey stock or canned chicken broth (include reserved stock) salt and pepper to taste**

Work in batches as necessary. In a large stockpot over medium heat, melt butter. Sauté onions until tender. Add thyme and flour and cook 3 to 5 minutes, stirring constantly. Stir in turkey stock or canned broth and simmer 15 minutes. Season with salt and pepper. Drain cranberries and stir into sauce. Gently stir in turkey chunks and simmer 15 more minutes. Divide evenly among tins. Cover with a sheet of plastic wrap, pressing down to cling to food. Apply board lid. Freeze.

Reheating Instructions

Defrost in refrigerator. Remove board lid and plastic wrap. Transfer to saucepan or microwave safe dish and heat thoroughly. Serve over stuffing or mashed potatoes.

Packaged mixes are a labor-saving option to homemade stuffing!

Herbed Stuffing

Makes 6, 12, or 18 4-serving sides

(approximately 1 cup per serving)

Ingredients and Instructions

24 servings	48 servings	72 servings	
3 pounds	6 pounds	9 pounds	crusty country style bread, cut into ½-inch cubes

Preheat oven to 325°. Work in batches as necessary. Spread bread cubes on cookie sheets. Toast in oven until dry (approximately 30 minutes). Stir midway during toasting for even browning.

1½ cups	3 cups	4½ cups	butter
8	16	24	medium onions, finely chopped
8	16	24	celery ribs, finely chopped

Work in batches as necessary. In a large skillet over medium heat, melt butter. Sauté onions and celery until tender. Remove from heat and set aside.

1 tablespoon	2 tablespoons	3 tablespoons	dried thyme
1½ teaspoons	1 tablespoon	1½ tablespoons	dried sage
1½ teaspoons	1 tablespoon	1½ tablespoons	dried rosemary
6 cups	12 cups	18 cups	chicken stock or canned broth
			salt and pepper to taste

In a large bowl, place toasted bread cubes, sautéed vegetables, dried herbs, and chicken stock or canned broth, stirring until evenly combined. Season with salt and pepper. Divide evenly among tins. Cover with a sheet of plastic wrap, pressing down to cling to food. Apply board lid. Freeze.

Baking Instructions

Defrost in refrigerator. Preheat oven to 350°. Remove board lid and plastic wrap. Cover loosely with foil to prevent drying. Bake until heated through and lightly browned (approximately 25 to 30 minutes).

Consider adding interest and flavor to stuffing with the following possibilities!

- Sauteed mushrooms
- Cooked, chopped bacon
- Chopped nuts (pecans, walnuts, hazelnuts, almonds)
- Chopped apple or pear
- Chopped dried fruit (cherries, cranberries, apricots, raisins, currants)

Roasted Turkey with Sage Gravy and Cornmeal Biscuit Mix

Makes 6, 12, or 18 4-serving meals

(approximately 1 cup per serving)

Divide and Conquer

- ◉ Strategize batch sizes based on available containers/cookware.
- ◉ Prepare biscuit mix.
- ◉ Roast turkey.
- ◉ Cut turkey into chunks.
- ◉ Chop and sauté vegetables.
- ◉ Prepare and label all packaging.

Look for fresh sage in your grocer's produce section. Do not substitute dried sage, as the flavor will be substantially altered.

Recommended Packaging

aluminum tins with board lids
freezer bags
plastic wrap

Ingredients and Instructions

6 meals 24 servings	12 meals 48 servings	18 meals 72 servings	
2	4	6	6 to 7 pound turkey breasts

Roast turkey breast. See *Preparing Turkey*. Cool. Debone and cut turkey into large chunks. Refrigerate. Reserve stock and reduce to taste.

¾ cup	1½ cups	2¼ cups	butter
3	6	9	medium leeks, white and light green part, thinly sliced
2 pounds	4 pounds	6 pounds	carrots, diced
6	12	18	celery ribs, diced
2 tablespoons	¼ cup	6 tablespoons	garlic, pressed or minced
24	48	72	fresh sage leaves, minced
4 teaspoons	8 teaspoons	¼ cup	dried thyme
1 cup	2 cups	3 cups	all-purpose flour
10 cups	20 cups	30 cups	turkey stock or canned chicken broth (include reserved stock)
2 cups	4 cups	6 cups	dry white wine
			salt and pepper to taste

Work in batches as necessary. In a large stockpot over medium heat, melt butter. Sauté leeks, carrots, and celery until tender. Add garlic, sage leaves, and thyme and cook 5 minutes. Stir in flour. Add wine and turkey stock or canned broth, stirring until evenly combined, and simmer 15 minutes. Season with salt and pepper. Gently stir in turkey chunks and simmer 15 more minutes. Divide evenly among tins. Cover with a sheet of plastic wrap, pressing down to cling to food. Apply board lid. Freeze.

Reheating Instructions

Defrost in refrigerator. Remove board lid and plastic wrap. Transfer to saucepan or microwave safe dish and heat thoroughly. Serve over biscuits or stuffing.

Cornmeal Biscuit Mix

Makes 24, 48, or 72 biscuits

24 biscuits	48 biscuits	72 biscuits	
4½ cups	9 cups	13½ cups	all-purpose flour
1 cup plus 2 tablespoons	2¼ cups	3 cups plus 6 tablespoons	yellow cornmeal
2 tablespoons	¼ cup	6 tablespoons	baking powder
2¼ teaspoons	4½ teaspoons	6¾ teaspoons	baking soda
2¼ teaspoons	4½ teaspoons	6¾ teaspoons	salt
1½ teaspoons	3 tablespoons	4½ tablespoons	sugar
1 cup plus 2 tablespoons	2¼ cups	3 cups plus 6 tablespoons	butter, chilled and cut into ½-inch pieces

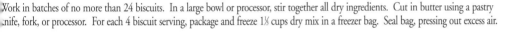

Work in batches of no more than 24 biscuits. In a large bowl or processor, stir together all dry ingredients. Cut in butter using a pastry knife, fork, or processor. For each 4 biscuit serving, package and freeze 1⅛ cups dry mix in a freezer bag. Seal bag, pressing out excess air.

Baking Instructions

Preheat oven to 450º. Bring mix to room temperature and place in bowl. For each 4 biscuit serving, add 6 tablespoons buttermilk. Stir gently until mixture forms a ball. On a lightly floured surface, pat into a square, approximately 1-inch thick. Cut into squares. Place on a baking sheet and bake until golden (approximately 15 minutes)

As an alternative to preparing a biscuit mix, supply group members with refrigerated or frozen biscuits.

Turkey-Bacon-Cheddar Loaf Kits

Makes 6, 12, or 18 4-serving meals

(¼ loaf per serving)

Divide and Conquer

- Strategize batch sizes based on available containers/cookware.
- Roast turkey.
- Cut turkey into chunks.
- Cook bacon.
- Package meat.
- Package frozen dough.
- Package cheese.
- Prepare and label all packaging.

Recommended Packaging

one gallon freezer bags
one quart freezer bags
snack bags
plastic wrap

Ingredients and Instructions

6 meals 24 servings	12 meals 48 servings	18 meals 72 servings	
6	**12**	**18**	**one pound loaves frozen bread dough**

Wrap each loaf of dough in foil or plastic wrap.

6 cups	**12 cups**	**18 cups**	**shredded cheddar cheese**

Package cheese in snack bags (1 cup per loaf).

1	**2**	**3**	**6 to 7 pound turkey breasts**

Cook turkey breast. See *Preparing Turkey*. Cool. Debone and cut turkey into chunks. Refrigerate. Reserve stock.

1½ cups	**3 cups**	**4½ cups**	**reserved turkey stock**
2 tablespoons	**¼ cup**	**6 tablespoons**	**cornstarch**
2 tablespoons	**¼ cup**	**6 tablespoons**	**water**

Simmer reserved stock over medium-high heat until reduced to required amounts (1½, 3, or 4½ cups). In a separate bowl, combine cornstarch and water. Slowly whisk cornstarch mixture into stock and continue simmering until slightly thickened. Pour stock mixture over turkey and stir gently to combine. Cool. Package in snack bags (1 cup per loaf). Refrigerate.

1½ pounds	**3 pounds**	**4½ pounds**	**bacon**

Work in batches as necessary. In a large skillet over medium heat (or in oven), cook bacon until crisp. Drain. Cool. Break each strip in half and divide evenly among snack bags. Place a loaf of frozen bread, a package of cheese, a package of turkey, and a package of bacon in each one gallon freezer bag. Include the following preparation instructions. Seal bag, pressing out excess air. Freeze.

Preparation Instructions

Remove bread from wrapping. Thaw in refrigerator (approximately 6 hours) and then set out to rise (approximately 1 to 2 hours). Or, thaw on counter (approximately 5 hours). Look for dough to double in bulk. Defrost cheese, turkey, and bacon in refrigerator. Roll dough approximately 10-inch x 14-inch. Scatter turkey down center of dough. Top with bacon strips and cheese. Using a knife, cut strips in dough on either side of filling. Alternating side to side, pull strips decoratively over filling (pinch end strips to seal). Cover and allow to rise again (approximately 45 minutes). Preheat oven to 350°. Bake approximately 40 minutes. If bread browns too quickly, cover with foil to halt browning.

Check freezer bags for off odors, which may transfer to foods. If an odor is present, allow bags to further "cure" by unsealing and airing until odor is no longer present.

Turkey Divan with Rice

Makes 6, 12, or 18 4-serving meals

(approximately 1½ cups per serving)

Recommended Packaging

aluminum tins with board lids
snack bags
plastic wrap

Ingredients and Instructions

6 meals 24 servings	12 meals 48 servings	18 meals 72 servings	
2	4	6	6 to 7 pound turkey breasts

Roast turkey breast. See *Preparing Turkey*. Cool. Debone and cut turkey into chunks. Refrigerate. Reserve stock and reduce to taste.

2 pounds	4 pounds	6 pounds	broccoli crowns

Cut broccoli into bite-sized pieces and steam until tender crisp.

2 pounds	4 pounds	6 pounds	long grain white rice

Prepare rice according to package directions and set aside.

4½ cups	9 cups	13½ cups	shredded sharp cheddar cheese

Package cheese in snack bags (¾ cup per meal or 3 tablespoons per serving).

1 cup	2 cups	3 cups	butter
1 cup	2 cups	3 cups	all-purpose flour
8 cups	16 cups	24 cups	turkey stock or canned chicken broth (include reserved stock)
8 cups	16 cups	24 cups	shredded sharp cheddar cheese
8 teaspoons	5 tablespoons plus 1 teaspoon	½ cup	Worcestershire sauce
4 pounds	8 pounds	12 pounds	sour cream salt and pepper to taste

Work in batches as necessary. In a large skillet over medium heat, melt butter. Stir in flour and cook 3 to 5 minutes. Slowly add turkey stock or canned broth stirring constantly until well blended. Whisk over medium heat until thickened. Add cheese and Worcestershire sauce, stirring until cheese is melted. Stir in sour cream. Remove from heat and transfer to a large container for combining ingredients. Add rice, broccoli, and turkey, stirring until evenly combined. Season with salt and pepper. Divide evenly among tins. Cool. Cover with sheet of plastic wrap, pressing down to cling to food. Place a package of cheese in each tin. Apply board lid. Freeze.

Divide and Conquer

- Strategize batch sizes based on available containers/cookware.
- Roast turkey.
- Cut turkey into chunks.
- Clean, chop, and steam broccoli.
- Package cheese.
- Prepare and label all packaging.

Reheating Instructions

Defrost in refrigerator. Remove board lid, cheese, and plastic wrap. Transfer to microwave safe dish and heat thoroughly. Alternatively, bake in container at 350° until heated through (approximately 30 minutes). During the last minutes of reheating, sprinkle with shredded cheese.

Have a turkey breast or two roasting in every corner. Use a large roaster in the oven, stockpots or large pans on the stovetop . . . and even the slow cooker on the counter. Give the slow cooker a running start.

Turkey Philly Loaf Kits

Makes 6, 12, or 18 4-serving meals

(¼ loaf per serving)

Recommended Packaging

one gallon freezer bags
one quart freezer bags
snack bags
plastic wrap

Divide and Conquer

- Strategize batch sizes based on available containers/cookware.
- Roast turkey.
- Cut turkey into chunks.
- Chop and sauté vegetables.
- Package vegetables.
- Package meat.
- Package frozen dough.
- Package cheese.
- Prepare and label all packaging.

Ingredients and Instructions

6 meals 24 servings	12 meals 48 servings	18 meals 72 servings	
6	12	18	one pound loaves frozen bread dough

Wrap each loaf of dough in foil or plastic wrap.

6 cups	12 cups	18 cups	shredded mozzarella cheese

Package cheese in snack bags (1 cup per loaf).

1	2	3	6 to 7 pound turkey breasts

Cook turkey breast. See *Preparing Turkey*. Cool. Debone and cut turkey into chunks. Refrigerate. Reserve stock.

1½ cups	3 cups	4½ cups	reserved stock
2 tablespoons	¼ cup	6 tablespoons	cornstarch
2 tablespoons	¼ cup	6 tablespoons	water

Simmer reserved stock over medium-high heat until reduced to required amounts (1½, 3, or 4½ cups). In a separate bowl, combine cornstarch and water. Slowly whisk cornstarch mixture into stock and continue simmering until slightly thickened. Pour stock mixture over turkey and stir gently to combine. Cool. Package in snack bags (1 cup per loaf).

			olive or vegetable oil
3	6	9	jumbo onions, cut into strips
3	6	9	large peppers (use any combination of red, yellow or green), cut into strips

In a large skillet or Dutch oven over medium heat, heat oil. Sauté onions until tender. Remove from pan and set aside. In same skillet, sauté peppers until tender crisp. Combine onions and peppers. Package onions and peppers in snack bags (approximately ¾ cup per loaf). Place a loaf of frozen bread, a package of cheese, a package of turkey, and a package of onion/peppers in each one gallon freezer bag. Include the following preparation instructions. Seal bag, pressing out excess air. Freeze.

Preparation Instructions:

Remove bread from wrapping. Thaw in refrigerator (approximately 6 hours) and then set out to rise (approximately 1 to 2 hours). Or, thaw on counter (approximately 5 hours). Look for dough to double in bulk. Defrost cheese, turkey, and onion/pepper mixture in refrigerator. Drain onion/pepper mixture well. Roll dough to approximately 10-inch x 14-inch. Scatter turkey down center of dough. Top with onions/peppers and cheese. Using a knife, cut strips in dough on either side of filling. Alternating side to side, pull strips decoratively over filling (pinch end strips to seal). Cover and allow to rise again (approximately 45 minutes). Preheat oven to 350°. Bake approximately 40 minutes. If bread browns too quickly, cover with foil to halt browning.

If you're a bread making (or bread machine) devotee, don't hesitate to make your own favorite loaves! Our loaf recipes include a one pound portion of frozen dough.

Turkey Pot Pie with Cornmeal Crust

Makes 6, 12, or 18 4-serving meals

(approximately 1½ cups per serving)

Recommended Packaging

aluminum tins with board lids
plastic wrap

Ingredients and Instructions

6 meals 24 servings	12 meals 48 servings	18 meals 72 servings	
3	6	9	**6 to 7 pound turkey breasts**

Roast turkey breast. See *Preparing Turkey*. Cool. Debone and cut turkey into chunks. Refrigerate. Reserve stock and reduce to taste.

			olive or vegetable oil
4	8	12	**medium onions, chopped**
2 pounds	4 pounds	6 pounds	**carrots, sliced or chopped finely**

Work in batches as necessary. In a large skillet over medium heat, heat oil. Sauté onions and carrots until tender. Remove from pan and set aside.

2½ cups	5 cups	7½ cups	**butter**
2½ cups	5 cups	7½ cups	**flour**
9 cups	18 cups	27 cups	**turkey stock or canned chicken broth (include reserved stock)**
7 cups	14 cups	21 cups	**milk**
2 tablespoons	¼ cup	6 tablespoons	**dried thyme**
1 tablespoon	2 tablespoons	3 tablespoons	**salt**
1¼ cups	2½ cups	3¾ cups	**dry white wine**
16 ounces	32 ounces	48 ounces	**frozen peas**

Work in batches as necessary. In a large skillet over medium heat, melt butter. Stir in flour and cook 3 to 5 minutes. Slowly add turkey stock or canned broth, milk, thyme, and salt, stirring constantly until well blended. Whisk over medium heat until thickened. Stir in wine and simmer 3 to 5 minutes. Remove from heat and transfer to a large container for combining ingredients. Stir in turkey and peas. Divide evenly among tins. Cover with a sheet of plastic wrap, pressing down to cling to food. Freeze overnight. Remove plastic wrap. Sprinkle cornmeal crust evenly on top of frozen pot pie. Press firmly into place. Cover with a sheet of plastic wrap, pressing down to cling to food. Apply board lid. Return to freezer.

Divide and Conquer

- Strategize batch sizes based on available containers/cookware.
- Prepare Cornmeal Crusts.
- Roast turkey.
- Cut turkey into chunks.
- Chop and sauté vegetables.
- Prepare and label all packaging.

Cornmeal Crust

crusts	12 crusts	18 crusts	
cups	12 cups	18 cups	all-purpose flour
cups	6 cups	9 cups	cornmeal
tablespoon	2 tablespoons	3 tablespoons	salt
teaspoons	4 teaspoons	2 tablespoons	baking powder
cups	4 cups	6 cups	butter or margarine
	12	18	small eggs, lightly beaten

Work in batches of no more than 6 crusts. In a large bowl, combine flour, cornmeal, salt, and baking powder.   Using a fork or pastry blender, cut butter into flour and cornmeal mixture until it resembles coarse crumbs. Add eggs, continuing to stir until a ball forms. Divide dough into desired number of crusts. Refrigerate.

Using a food processor, work in batches of 2 crusts each (dividing the 6 crust ingredient list). Place dry ingredients and butter in processor bowl with metal blade. Process until mixture resembles coarse crumbs.   Add eggs through feed tube, processing until a ball forms.   Divide each ball into 2 crusts. Refrigerate.

Reheating Instructions

Defrost in refrigerator. Preheat oven to 375°. Remove board lid and plastic wrap. Cover loosely with foil to prevent drying. Bake until bubbly around the edges and hot in the center (approximately 40 minutes). Let stand 15 minutes before cutting.

In the absence of a jumbo container to mix ingredients, consider mixing in your packaging. This may also help portion ingredients more evenly. For Turkey Pot Pie, mix 2 cups cooked turkey, 2 cups sauce, and ½ cup peas in each container. Cover with crust.

Turkey with Wild Rice and Almonds

Makes 6, 12, or 18 4-serving meals

(approximately 1½ cups per serving)

Divide and Conquer

- Strategize batch sizes based on available containers/cookware.
- Roast turkey.
- Cut turkey into chunks.
- Chop and sauté onions.
- Package almonds.
- Prepare and label all packaging.

Your local health food store may be a great resource for bulk grains, nuts, legumes, and dried fruits at fabulous prices!

Recommended Packaging

aluminum tins with board lids
snack bags
plastic wrap

Ingredients and Instructions

6 meals 24 servings	12 meals 48 servings	18 meals 72 servings	
2	4	6	7 to 8 pound turkey breasts

Roast turkey breast. See *Preparing Turkey*. Cool. Debone and cut turkey into chunks. Refrigerate. Reserve stock and reduce to taste.

1½ cups	3 cups	4½ cups	slivered almonds

Package almonds in snack bags (¼ cup per meal or 1 tablespoon per serving).

½ cup	1 cup	1½ cups	butter
3	6	9	medium onions, chopped
2½ cups	5 cups	7½ cups	wild rice, washed
2½ cups	5 cups	7½ cups	brown rice
12 cups	24 cups	36 cups	turkey stock or canned chicken broth
8 cups	16 cups	24 cups	heavy cream
¾ cup	1½ cups	2¼ cups	dry sherry or white wine (or 6, 12, or 18 tablespoons fresh lemon juice)
1 tablespoon	2 tablespoons	3 tablespoons	salt
2 teaspoons	4 teaspoons	2 tablespoons	ground black pepper

Work in batches as necessary. In a large skillet over medium heat, melt butter. Sauté onions until lightly browned. In a buttered roaster, combine rice, onions, and all remaining ingredients except turkey. Cover and bake 1½ hours at 325°. Remove cover and bake uncovered until sauce reduces to desired level, approximately ½ hour. Stir in turkey chunks. Divide evenly among tins. Cool. Cover with a sheet of plastic wrap, pressing down to cling to food. Place a bag of almonds in each tin. Apply board lid. Freeze.

Reheating Instructions

Defrost in refrigerator. Remove board lid, almonds, and plastic wrap. Transfer to microwave safe dish and heat thoroughly. Alternatively, bake in container at 350° until heated through (approximately 30 minutes). Stir in almonds.

Miscellaneous

Black Bean Burritos
Vegetable Barley Stew
Lentil Chili
Lasagna Primavera
Stuffed Pasta Shells
Vegetable Lasagna with a Red Sauce
Scalloped Potatoes with Ham
Quiche Lorraine
Pizza Kits

(See also Going Beyond Entrée Recipes – Soup's On)

Black Bean Burritos

Makes 6, 12, or 18 4-serving meals

(1½ burritos per serving)

Recommended Packaging

aluminum tins with board lids
plastic wrap

Ingredients and Instructions

6 meals 24 servings	12 meals 48 servings	18 meals 72 servings	
3½ pounds	7 pounds	10½ pounds	dried black beans or
13 pounds	26 pounds	39 pounds	canned black beans, drained and rinsed

In a large stockpot, soak beans overnight. Drain and rinse. Return to stockpot, cover with water and simmer 1 hour or until desired tenderness. Drain and set aside.

			olive or vegetable oil
7	14	21	medium onions, finely chopped
2 tablespoons plus 1 teaspoon	4 tablespoons plus 2 teaspoons	7 tablespoons	garlic, pressed or minced
7	14	21	jalapeno peppers, seeded and diced
7 pounds	14 pounds	21 pounds	canned diced tomatoes, undrained
2 tablespoons plus 1 teaspoon	4 tablespoons plus 2 teaspoons	7 tablespoons	chili powder
2 tablespoons plus 1 teaspoon	4 tablespoons plus 2 teaspoons	7 tablespoons	ground cumin
2 tablespoons plus 1 teaspoon	4 tablespoons plus 2 teaspoons	7 tablespoons	dried oregano
3	6	9	lemons, sliced and seeded
2 teaspoons	4 teaspoons	2 tablespoons	salt

Work in batches as necessary. In a large stockpot over medium heat, heat oil. Sauté onions, garlic, and jalapeno peppers until tender. Stir in drained beans, tomatoes, chili powder, cumin, oregano, lemon slices, and salt (omit if using canned beans) and bring to a boil at high heat. Reduce heat, cover, and simmer 30 minutes. Remove cover and simmer until slightly thickened (approximately 20 minutes). Remove lemon slices. Working in batches as necessary, puree half of bean mixture in a blender or food processor until smooth. Add unblended bean mixture to blended and stir thoroughly. Cool.

48 ounces	96 ounces	9 pounds	mild salsa or picante sauce
6 cups	12 cups	18 cups	shredded Monterey Jack or Co-Jack cheese
36	72	108	10-inch flour tortillas

Package salsa in snack bags (1 cup per meal or ¼ cup per serving). Package cheese in snack bags (1 cup per meal or ¼ cup per serving).

Divide and Conquer

- ☞ Strategize batch sizes based on available containers/cookware.
- ☞ Soak beans.
- ☞ Cook beans.
- ☞ Chop and sauté vegetables.
- ☞ Package salsa.
- ☞ Package cheese.
- ☞ Prepare and label all packaging.

Assemble burritos by placing ½ cup bean mixture onto each tortilla, folding ends in, and rolling. Place 6 burritos (or 1½ per serving) in each tin. Cover with a sheet of plastic wrap, pressing down to cling to food. Place a package of salsa and a package of cheese in each tin. Apply board lid. Freeze.

Reheating Instructions

Defrost in refrigerator. Preheat oven to 350°. Remove board lid, salsa, cheese, and plastic wrap. Transfer to baking dish, if desired, or bake in aluminum tin. Spread salsa over burritos. Cover loosely with foil to prevent drying. Bake until bubbly around the edges and hot in the center (approximately 30 minutes). Remove foil and sprinkle with cheese during last 5 minutes of baking. Let stand at room temperature 5 minutes before serving.

Adapt Black Bean Burritos for meat lovers by adding ground beef, ground sausage, or grilled chicken.

Divide and Conquer

- ◉ Strategize batch sizes based on available containers/cookware.
- ◉ Chop and sauté onions.
- ◉ Chop carrots.
- ◉ Prepare and label all packaging.

Speed cooling of hot foods by dividing into smaller portions. Or, place pot in a kitchen sink ice bath. Stir frequently.

Vegetable Barley Stew

Makes 6, 12, or 18 4-serving meals

(approximately 1½ cups per serving)

Recommended Packaging

freezer bags or aluminum tins with board lids
plastic wrap

Ingredients and Instructions

6 meals 24 servings	12 meals 48 servings	18 meals 72 servings	
			olive or vegetable oil
4	8	12	medium onions, chopped
6 pounds	12 pounds	18 pounds	canned diced tomatoes, undrained
12 cups	24 cups	36 cups	canned vegetable or beef broth
2 pounds	4 pounds	6 pounds	carrots, cut into 1-inch pieces
1 cup	2 cups	3 cups	pearl barley
2	4	6	bay leaves
1 tablespoon	2 tablespoons	3 tablespoons	dried thyme

Work in batches as necessary. In a large stockpot over medium heat, heat oil. Sauté onions until tender. Stir in tomatoes, canned vegetable or beef broth, carrots, barley, bay leaves, and thyme and bring to a boil. Reduce heat and simmer, uncovered, until barley is tender (approximately 1 hour).

16 ounces	32 ounces	48 ounces	frozen corn
16 ounces	32 ounces	48 ounces	frozen green beans
16 ounces	32 ounces	48 ounces	frozen peas
			salt and pepper to taste

Add corn, beans, and peas and simmer 15 minutes. If stew is too thick, add water or broth, 1 cup at a time, until desired consistency is reached. Season with salt and pepper. Cool. Divide evenly among freezer bags. Seal bags, pressing out excess air. Freeze.

Reheating Instructions

Defrost in refrigerator. Transfer to saucepan or microwave safe and heat thoroughly.

Lentil Chili

Makes 6, 12, or 18 4-serving meals
(approximately 1½ cups per serving)

Recommended Packaging   freezer bags or aluminum tins with board lids
plastic wrap

Ingredients and Instructions

meals 4 servings	12 meals 48 servings	18 meals 72 servings	
			olive or vegetable oil
	6	9	large onions, chopped
	6	9	red bell peppers, seeded and chopped
	6	9	green bell peppers, seeded and chopped
2	24	36	green onions, chopped
tablespoon	2 tablespoons	3 tablespoons	garlic, pressed or minced
pounds	6 pounds	9 pounds	lentils, rinsed
0 lbs, 8 oz	21 pounds	31 lbs, 8 oz	canned crushed tomatoes
2 ounces	84 ounces	7 lbs, 8 oz	canned diced tomatoes, undrained
½ cups	9 cups	13½ cups	water
tablespoons	¾ cup	1 cup plus 2 tablespoons	chili powder
tablespoons	¼ cup	6 tablespoons	dried marjoram
tablespoons	¼ cup	6 tablespoons	dried oregano
tablespoons	¼ cup	6 tablespoons	dried basil
tablespoons	¼ cup	6 tablespoons	salt
tablespoon	2 tablespoons	3 tablespoons	ground black pepper

Work in batches as necessary. In a large stockpot over medium-high heat, heat oil. Sauté onions, peppers, and garlic until tender. Stir in lentils, tomatoes, water, and spices and simmer, stirring occasionally, until lentils are tender (approximately 1 hour).

cups	6 cups	9 cups	shredded Parmesan cheese

Stir in Parmesan cheese. Continue simmering, uncovered, until mixture is thick (approximately 30 minutes). Remove from heat. Cool. Divide evenly among freezer bags. Seal bag, pressing out excess air. Freeze.

Reheating Instructions

Defrost in refrigerator. Remove board lid and plastic wrap. Transfer to saucepan or microwave safe dish and heat thoroughly.

Divide and Conquer
- Strategize batch sizes based on available containers/cookware.
- Chop and sauté vegetables.
- Prepare and label all packaging.

For added interest and color, include a variety of lentils in Lentil Chili. Cook until all are tender.

Lasagna Primavera

Makes 6, 12, or 18 4-serving meals

(approximately 1½ cups per serving)

Recommended Packaging

5" x 12" or 8" x 8" (6-cup) aluminum tins
with board lids
snack bags
plastic wrap

Ingredients and Instructions

6 meals 24 servings	12 meals 48 servings	18 meals 72 servings	
1½ cups	3 cups	4½ cups	butter
3	6	9	medium onions, finely chopped
2 teaspoons	4 teaspoons	2 tablespoons	garlic, pressed or minced
1½ cups	3 cups	4½ cups	all-purpose flour
6 cups	12 cups	18 cups	chicken stock or canned broth
6 cups	12 cups	18 cups	milk
6 cups	12 cups	18 cups	shredded mozzarella cheese
1½ cups	3 cups	4½ cups	shredded Parmesan cheese
2 tablespoons	¼ cup	6 tablespoons	dried basil
1 tablespoon	2 tablespoons	3 tablespoons	dried oregano
1 tablespoon	2 tablespoon	3 tablespoons	salt
2 teaspoons	4 teaspoons	2 tablespoons	ground black pepper

Work in batches as necessary. In a large stockpot over medium heat, melt butter. Add onions and garlic and sauté until tender. Stir in flour and cook 3 to 5 minutes. Slowly add chicken stock or canned broth and milk, stirring constantly until well blended. Whisk over medium heat until thickened. Remove from heat. Add mozzarella and Parmesan cheeses, stirring until cheeses melt. Stir in basil, oregano, salt, and pepper. Set aside.

12 cups	24 cups	36 cups	vegetables and mushrooms of choice

Chop or dice vegetables into small pieces. In a large stock pot, blanch or lightly steam summer squash, zucchini, carrots, asparagus, cauliflower, or broccoli. Slice mushrooms and lightly sauté. Thoroughly drain frozen spinach, and squeeze to remove excess liquid. Fresh spinach may be washed, dried, and layered in the lasagna.

1½ cups	3 cups	4½ cups	shredded Parmesan cheese

Package cheese in snack bags (¼ cup per meal or 1 tablespoon per serving).

Divide and Conquer

- Strategize batch sizes based on available containers/cookware.
- Chop vegetables.
- Cook vegetables.
- Package cheese.
- Prepare and label all packaging.

Size Adjuster (9" x 13")

Package cheese in snack bags (6 tablespoons per meal or 1 tablespoon per serving).

6	72	108	lasagna noodles, slightly undercooked
½ pounds	3 pounds	4½ pounds	ricotta cheese
cups	12 cups	18 cups	shredded mozzarella cheese

ightly spray each tin with nonstick cooking spray. Spread ½ cup (or 2 tablespoons per serving) of sauce on bottom of each tin. Cover auce with a layer of noodles. Divide and spread half of ricotta cheese evenly among tins. Divide and spread half of mozzarella cheese venly among tins. Spread 1 cup (or ¼ cup per serving) vegetables/mushroom mixture over cheeses. Spread 1 cup (or ¼ cup per serving) auce over vegetables/mushroom mixture. Repeat. Top with a final layer of noodles and ½ cup (or 2 tablespoons per serving) sauce. Cover ith a sheet of plastic wrap, pressing down to cling to food. Place a package of cheese in each tin. Apply board lid. Freeze.

Size Adjuster (9" x 13")

Lightly spray each tin with nonstick cooking spray. Spread ¾ cup (or 2 tablespoons per serving) of sauce on bottom of each tin. Cover sauce with a layer of noodles. Divide and spread half of ricotta cheese evenly among tins. Divide and spread half of mozzarella cheese evenly among tins. Spread 1½ cups (or ¼ cup per serving) vegetables/mushroom mixture over cheeses. Spread 1½ cups (or ¼ cup per serving) sauce over vegetables/mushroom mixture. Repeat. Top with a final layer of noodles and ¾ cup (or 2 tablespoons per serving) sauce. Cover with a sheet of plastic wrap, pressing down to cling to food. Place a package of cheese in each tin. Apply board lid. Freeze.

Reheating Instructions

Defrost in refrigerator. Preheat oven to 350°. Remove board lid and plastic wrap. Cover loosely with foil to prevent drying. Bake until ubbly around the edges and hot in center (approximately 30 to 40 minutes). Remove foil and sprinkle with Parmesan cheese during last 5 inutes of baking. Let stand 15 minutes before cutting.

Size Adjuster

6 Meal Equivalents	12 Meal Equivalents	18 Meal Equivalents
(6) 5" x 12" or 8" x 8"	(12) 5" x 12" or 8" x 8"	(18) 5" x 12" or 8" x 8"
(4) 9" x 13"	(8) 9" x 13"	(12) 9" x 13"

Stuffed Pasta Shells

Makes 6, 12, or 18 4-serving meals

(4 shells per serving)

Recommended Packaging

aluminum tins with board lids
snack bags
plastic wrap

Ingredients and Instructions

6 meals	12 meals	18 meals	
24 servings	48 servings	72 servings	

Tomato Sauce

2	4	6	medium onions, finely chopped
1½ teaspoons	1 tablespoon	4½ teaspoons	garlic, pressed or minced
5 tablespoons	½ cup plus 2 tablespoons	¾ cup plus 3 tablespoons	dried parsley
1½ tablespoons	3 tablespoons	4½ tablespoons	dried basil
1 tablespoon	2 tablespoons	3 tablespoons	dried oregano
6	12	18	bay leaves
1 teaspoon	2 teaspoons	1 tablespoon	ground black pepper
72 ounces	9 pounds	13 lbs, 8 oz	canned tomato sauce
24 ounces	48 ounces	72 ounces	canned chopped tomatoes, undrained

Place all the ingredients in a large stockpot. Cover and bring to a boil. Uncover, reduce heat, and simmer, stirring occasionally, 1 hour. Remove from heat and set aside.

1½ cups	3 cups	4½ cups	shredded Parmesan cheese

Package cheese in snack bags (¼ cup per meal or 1 tablespoon per serving).

3	6	9	12-ounce packages jumbo shells, slightly undercooked
6	12	18	eggs, lightly beaten
6 pounds	12 pounds	18 pounds	ricotta cheese
6 cups	12 cups	18 cups	shredded mozzarella cheese
2½ cups	5 cups	7½ cups	shredded Parmesan cheese
½ cup	1 cup	1½ cups	dried parsley
1 tablespoon	2 tablespoons	3 tablespoons	salt
1½ teaspoons	1 tablespoon	4½ teaspoons	ground black pepper

Divide and Conquer

- ❧ Strategize batch sizes based on available containers/cookware.
- ❧ Prepare tomato sauce.
- ❧ Assemble ricotta filling.
- ❧ Package cheese.
- ❧ Prepare and label all packaging.

In a large bowl, beat eggs. Stir in cheeses, parsley, salt, and pepper until evenly combined. Spoon approximately 2 tablespoons cheese mixture into each shell. Arrange shells (4 per serving) in tins. Pour sauce (½ cup per serving) over shells. Cover with a sheet of plastic wrap, pressing down to cling to food. Place a package of cheese in tin. Apply board lid. Freeze.

Reheating Instructions

Defrost in refrigerator. Preheat oven to 350°. Remove board lid, cheese, and plastic wrap. Bake until bubbly (approximately 40 minutes). During the last 5 minutes of baking, sprinkle with Parmesan cheese.

Vegetable Lasagna with a Red Sauce

Makes 6, 12, or 18 4-serving meals

(approximately 1½ cups per serving)

Recommended Packaging

5" x 12" or 8" x 8" (6-cup) aluminum tins
with board lids
snack bags
plastic wrap

Ingredients and Instructions

6 meals 24 servings	12 meals 48 servings	18 meals 72 servings	
Tomato Sauce			
3	6	9	medium onions, finely chopped
2 teaspoons	4 teaspoons	2 tablespoons	garlic, pressed or minced
6 tablespoons	¾ cup	1 cup plus 2 tablespoons	dried parsley
2½ tablespoons	5 tablespoons	7½ tablespoons	dried basil
1½ tablespoons	3 tablespoons	4½ tablespoons	dried oregano
9	18	27	bay leaves
1½ teaspoons	1 tablespoon	1½ tablespoons	ground black pepper
72 ounces	9 pounds	13 lbs, 8 oz	canned tomato sauce
72 ounces	9 pounds	13 lbs, 8 oz	canned chopped tomatoes, undrained

Place all ingredients in a large stockpot. Cover and bring to a boil. Uncover, reduce heat, and simmer, stirring occasionally, 1 hour. Remove from heat and set aside.

12 cups	24 cups	36 cups	vegetables and mushrooms of choice

Chop or dice vegetables into small pieces. In a large stockpot, blanch or lightly steam summer squash, zucchini, carrots, asparagus, cauliflower, or broccoli. Slice mushrooms and lightly sauté. Thoroughly drain frozen spinach and squeeze to remove excess liquid. Fresh spinach may be washed, dried, and layered in the lasagna.

1½ cups	3 cups	4½ cups	shredded Parmesan cheese

Package cheese in snack bags (¼ cup per meal or 1 tablespoon per serving)

Divide and Conquer

- Strategize batch sizes based on available containers/cookware.
- Prepare sauce.
- Chop vegetables.
- Cook vegetables.
- Package cheese.
- Prepare and label all packaging.

Package cheese in snack bags (6 tablespoons per meal or 1 tablespoon per serving).

36	72	108	lasagna noodles, slightly undercooked
1½ pounds	3 pounds	4½ pounds	ricotta cheese
9 cups	18 cups	27 cups	shredded mozzarella cheese

Lightly spray each tin with nonstick cooking spray. Spread ½ cup (or 2 tablespoons per serving) of sauce on bottom of each tin. Cover sauce with a layer of noodles. Divide and spread ricotta cheese evenly among tins. Divide and spread mozzarella cheese evenly among tins. Spread 1 cup (or ¼ cup per serving) vegetables/mushroom mixture over cheeses. Spread 1 cup (or ¼ cup per serving) sauce over vegetables/mushroom mixture. Repeat. Top with a final layer of noodles and ½ cup (or 2 tablespoons per serving) sauce. Cover with a sheet of plastic wrap, pressing down to cling to food. Place a package of cheese in each tin. Apply board lid. Freeze.

Lightly spray each tin with nonstick cooking spray. Spread ¾ cup (or 2 tablespoons per serving) of sauce on bottom of each tin. Cover sauce with a layer of noodles. Divide and spread ricotta cheese evenly among tins. Divide and spread mozzarella cheese evenly among tins. Spread 1½ cups (or ¼ cup per serving) vegetables/mushroom mixture over cheeses. Spread 1½ cups (or ¼ cup per serving) sauce over vegetables/mushroom mixture. Repeat. Top with a final layer of noodles and ¾ cup (or 2 tablespoons per serving) sauce. Cover with a sheet of plastic wrap, pressing down to cling to food. Place a package of cheese in each tin. Apply board lid. Freeze.

Reheating Instructions

Defrost in refrigerator. Preheat oven to 350°. Remove board lid, cheese, and plastic wrap. Cover loosely with foil to prevent drying. Bake until bubbly around the edges and hot in center (approximately 30 to 40 minutes). Remove foil and sprinkle with Parmesan cheese during last 5 minutes of baking. Let stand 15 minutes before cutting.

Size Adjuster		
6 Meal Equivalents	12 Meal Equivalents	18 Meal Equivalents
(6) 5" x 12" or 8" x 8"	(12) 5" x 12" or 8" x 8"	(18) 5" x 12" or 8" x 8"
(4) 9" x 13"	(8) 9" x 13"	(12) 9" x 13"

Scalloped Potatoes with Ham

Makes 6, 12, or 18 4-serving meals

(approximately 1½ cups per serving)

Divide and Conquer

- Strategize batch sizes based on available containers/cookware.
- Cut ham into chunks.
- Prepare cheese sauce.
- Prepare and label all packaging.

Recommended Packaging

aluminum tins with board lids
plastic wrap

Ingredients and Instructions

6 meals	12 meals	18 meals	
24 servings	48 servings	72 servings	
9 pounds	**18 pounds**	**27 pounds**	cooked ham, cut into chunks
10 pounds	**20 pounds**	**30 pounds**	potatoes, peeled and sliced ¼-inch thick

Refrigerate chunked ham. In a large stockpot, bring salted water to boil. Add potatoes. Return to boil, reduce heat, and simmer until potatoes are softened, yet firm (approximately 15 to 20 minutes). Drain potatoes. Set aside.

1 cup	2 cups	3 cups	butter
1	2	3	onions, finely chopped
1 cup	2 cups	3 cups	all-purpose flour
6 cups	12 cups	18 cups	milk, scalded
2 cups	4 cups	6 cups	chicken stock or canned broth
8 cups	16 cups	24 cups	shredded sharp cheddar cheese
			salt and pepper to taste
1½ cups	3 cups	4½ cups	breadcrumbs

Work in batches as necessary. In a large stockpot over medium heat, melt butter. Add onion and sauté until tender. Stir in flour and cook 3 to 5 minutes. Slowly add scalded milk and chicken stock or canned broth, whisking to combine. Continue whisking over medium heat until thickened. Remove from heat. Stir in cheese until melted. Season with salt and pepper. Divide half of potatoes and then half of ham evenly among tins. Divide and spread half of cheese sauce evenly among tins. Repeat. Divide and sprinkle breadcrumbs evenly among tins. Cool. Cover with a sheet of plastic wrap, pressing down to cling to food. Apply board lid. Freeze.

Baking Instructions

Defrost in refrigerator. Preheat oven to 350°. Remove board lid and plastic wrap. Bake until potatoes are tender (approximately 40 minutes). Cover loosely with foil to halt browning if necessary.

Quiche Lorraine

Makes 6, 12, or 18 4-serving meals

(¼ quiche per serving)

Recommended Packaging

frozen pie shells in aluminum pie tins
one gallon freezer bags
foil
plastic wrap

Ingredients and Instructions

6 meals	12 meals	18 meals	
24 servings	48 servings	72 servings	
	12	18	frozen pie shells
6 cups	12 cups	18 cups	shredded Swiss cheese
1½ pounds	3 pounds	4½ pounds	ham, chopped in ¼-inch cubes
24	48	72	eggs
12 cups	24 cups	36 cups	half and half
1 teaspoon	2 teaspoons	1 tablespoon	ground black pepper
6 tablespoons	¾ cup	1 cup plus 2 tablespoons	chopped chives

Preheat oven to 375°. In a large bowl, beat together eggs and half and half. Stir in pepper. Divide ham and cheese evenly among pie shells. Pour egg mixture over cheese, dividing evenly among pie shells. Sprinkle each quiche with 1 tablespoon chives. Swirl with spoon to submerge. Bake until knife inserted in center comes out clean (approximately 30 to 40 minutes). Cool completely. Wrap with plastic wrap and foil. Place in freezer bag. Seal bag, pressing out excess air. Freeze.

Reheating Instructions

Defrost in refrigerator. Preheat oven to 375°. Remove packaging. Reheat until heated through (approximately 30 minutes). Cover loosely with foil to halt browning if necessary.

Divide and Conquer

- Strategize batch sizes based on available containers/cookware.
- Cube ham.
- Prepare and label all packaging.

Vary quiche fillings to include your favorite meats and cheeses.

Pizza Kits

Makes 6, 12, or 18 4-serving meals (2 pizzas per meal)
(approximately ½ of 10-inch pizza per serving)

Recommended Packaging

two gallon freezer bags
one gallon freezer bags
snack bags (for sauce and toppings)
sandwich bags (for cheese)
plastic wrap

Divide and Conquer

- Strategize batch sizes based on available containers/cookware.
- Prepare crusts.
- Prepare tomato sauce.
- Package tomato sauce.
- Package cheese.
- Package toppings.
- Prepare and label all packaging.

Ingredients and Instructions

6 meals 24 servings	12 meals 48 servings	18 meals 72 servings	

Shopping List for Crust

6	**12**	**18**	**packages dry yeast**
16 cups	**32 cups**	**48 cups**	**all-purpose flour (approximate measurements)**
¾ cup	**1½ cups**	**2¼ cups**	**olive oil**
1½ teaspoons	**1 tablespoon**	**4½ teaspoons**	**salt**

Crust

Working in batches, prepare and pre-bake pizza crusts. Each batch will make 6 10-inch to 12-inch pizza crusts.

Prepare 2 batches of the following:	Prepare 4 batches of the following:	Prepare 6 batches of the following:	
3 cups			**lukewarm water**
3			**packages dry yeast**
7½ to 9 cups			**all-purpose flour**
6 tablespoons			**olive oil**
¾ teaspoon			**salt**

In a large bowl, combine water, yeast, and 4½ cups of flour. Mix well. Add oil, salt, and remaining flour as needed. Work ingredients together until dough holds its shape. Place dough on a lightly floured surface and knead until smooth and elastic (approximately 5 minutes). Transfer to a lightly oiled bowl. Cover with plastic wrap or a kitchen towel, and let rest until doubled in size (approximately 1 hour). Remove to slightly floured surface. Cut into 6 equal portions. Form each into a smooth ball and cover with a towel. Preheat oven to 450° Lightly oil baking sheets and sprinkle with cornmeal. On a well-floured surface, roll or press each ball into a 10-inch to 12-inch crust. Transfer to baking sheets, prick with a fork, and bake 4 minutes. Cool. Wrap each crust in plastic wrap and bag in a two gallon freezer bag Seal bag, pressing out excess air. Freeze.

Pizza Sauce

4 ounces	10 lbs, 8 oz	15 lbs, 12 oz	crushed tomatoes
teaspoons	4 teaspoons	2 tablespoons	garlic, pressed or minced
tablespoon	2 tablespoons	3 tablespoons	dried oregano
tablespoon	2 tablespoons	3 tablespoons	dried basil
	6	9	bay leaves
			pepper to taste

Place all the ingredients in a large stockpot. Cover and bring to a boil. Uncover, reduce heat, and simmer, stirring occasionally, 30 minutes. Remove and discard bay leaves. Remove from heat. Cool. Package sauce in snack bags (approximately ¾ cup per pizza).

8 cups	36 cups	54 cups	shredded mozzarella cheese

Package cheese in sandwich bags (1½ cups per pizza).

For each meal, place 2 packages of sauce and 2 packages of cheese in each one gallon freezer bag. Add bags of freezer friendly toppings, as desired. Seal bag, pressing out excess air. Freeze. Purchase and supply canned toppings, as desired.

Baking Instructions

Defrost in refrigerator. Preheat oven to 450°. Remove packaging. Place crust on lightly oiled baking sheet. Assemble toppings. Bake until cheese bubbles (approximately 10 minutes).

Freezer Friendly Toppings
- Browned ground beef
- Chopped green, yellow, or red pepper
- Browned Italian sausage
- Sliced mushrooms
- Pepperoni
- Pine nuts
- Prosciutto
- Grilled vegetables
- Grilled chicken
- Caramelized onions
- Roasted red pepper
- Feta cheese

Canned Toppings
- Anchovies
- Black or green olives
- Artichoke hearts
- Sun dried tomatoes

Chapter 5

Beyond Entrée Recipes

Beyond Entrée Recipes

You will find that, over time, *Cooking Among Friends®* radically changes the way you cook. Once you discover the freedom of having prepared dinner entrées in the freezer, you'll be gripped by a desire to bring the same kind of efficiency to breakfast, lunch, snacks, appetizers, side items, and desserts. Preparing single batches suddenly becomes clearly inefficient. If you're preparing a freezer-friendly, family-favorite food item, why not prepare two or three extra and freeze?

You will also be repeatedly impressed by the financial advantages of bulk buying. You may be introduced to items that you previously did not realize were available in bulk. Suddenly, preparing your own marinades and sauces, and stirring together your own dry mixes, seems sensible and easy. Especially when you can share them among your group.

This collection of recipes has been included not only to provide possible food exchange recipes, but also to provide possible fill-your-freezer recipes. We hope they remind you of your own family favorites, provide an indicator for types of foods that freeze well, and inspire you toward the possibilities. May your family members and guests be delightfully, and relatively effortlessly, lavished in your home.

Please note that Beyond Entrée recipe yields vary considerably with consideration given to ease of multiplying or dividing ingredients, and ease of preparation.

Baked Goods

Buttermilk Biscuits
Dinner Rolls
Caramel Pecan Rolls
Pumpkin Bread
Zucchini Bread

Buttermilk Biscuits

24 biscuits

1	package dry yeast
¼ cup	lukewarm water
2 cups	buttermilk

In a small bowl, dissolve yeast in lukewarm water. Add buttermilk. Set aside.

5 cups	all-purpose flour
3 tablespoons	sugar
1 tablespoon	baking powder
1 teaspoon	baking soda
2 teaspoons	salt
¾ cup	vegetable shortening

Preheat oven to 425°. In a large mixing bowl, whisk together dry ingredients. Cut in vegetable shortening. Add buttermilk mixture, stirring to combine. Place on a lightly floured surface and knead briefly. Roll dough to ½-inch thickness, forming an even square. Using a pizza cutter, cut into an even grid of 25 square biscuits. Alternatively, cut with a biscuit cutter, rerolling dough until all is used. Place biscuits on a greased baking sheet. Cover and let rise 1 hour. Bake until lightly browned (approximately 8 minutes). Portion as desired and place in freezerr bags. Seal bags, pressing out excess air. Freeze.

Dinner Rolls

48 rolls

3	packages dry yeast
1½ cups	lukewarm water
1½ cups	lukewarm milk
1 cup	sugar
3 teaspoons	salt
3	eggs, slightly beaten
1 cup	butter, melted and cooled
11 to 12 cups	all-purpose flour

In a small bowl, dissolve yeast in lukewarm water. In a large mixing bowl, combine yeast mixture, milk, sugar, salt, eggs, and butter. Beat well with a spoon. Add 6 cups of flour, continuing to beat well with a spoon. Continue adding flour, 1 cup at a tim until dough is soft but elastic. On a floured surface, knead dough well. Divide into equal portions. Divide each portion into 8 dinner rolls and shape as desired. Place rolls in tins. Cover with a sheet of plastic wrap, pressing down to cling to food. App board lid. Place an expiration date of one month following freezing on baking instru tions. Freeze.

Baking Instructions

Defrost. Allow to rise. Preheat oven to 400°. Bake until browned (approximately 1 to 15 minutes). For best results, use by _____.

Caramel Pecan Rolls

48 rolls

	packages dry yeast
cup	lukewarm water
¼ cups	milk
cup	sugar
teaspoons	salt
	eggs, slightly beaten
cup	vegetable shortening, melted and cooled
0 to 11 cups	all-purpose flour

n a small bowl, dissolve yeast in lukewarm water. In a large mixing bowl, combine east mixture, milk, sugar, salt, eggs, and shortening. Beat well with a spoon. Add 6 ups of flour, continuing to beat well with a spoon. Continue adding flour, 1 cup at a me, until dough is soft but elastic. On a floured surface, knead dough well. Divide nto 6 equal portions. Cover and let rise.

½ cups	butter, softened
½ cups	brown sugar, packed
½ cups	nuts, chopped

n a medium bowl, blend together butter, brown sugar, and nuts for filling. Set aside.

½ cups	butter, softened
½ cups	brown sugar, packed
½ cups	nuts, chopped
tablespoons	light corn syrup

n another bowl, blend together butter, brown sugar, nuts, and corn syrup. Divide venly among tins, spreading to coat bottom. Assemble rolls. Roll each portion into a ectangle. Spread with divided filling. Roll tightly, beginning at the wide side. Cut ach log into 8 rolls. Place rolls in tins. Cover with a sheet of plastic wrap, pressing own to cling to food. Apply board lid. Freeze. Place an expiration date of one nonth following freezing on baking instructions.

Baking Instructions

Defrost. Allow to rise. Preheat oven to 350°. Bake until browned (approximately 20 to 25 minutes). For best results, use by _____.

A dd your favorite flavors to Caramel Pecan Rolls. Consider cinnamon, nutmeg, orange zest, and lemon zest.

Pumpkin Bread

(6) 8-inch loaves

5¼ cups	all-purpose flour
1 tablespoon	baking soda
1 tablespoon	cinnamon
1½ teaspoons	salt
1½ teaspoons	nutmeg
¾ teaspoon	ground cloves

Preheat oven to 350º. In a large mixing bowl, stir together dry ingredients. Set aside.

1½ cups	butter, softened
3 cups	brown sugar, packed
6	eggs
3 cups	pureed pumpkin
2 cups	semi-sweet chocolate mini morsels
1½ cups	walnuts or pecans, chopped

In another large bowl, cream butter and sugar. Add eggs and beat well. Add dry ingredients alternating with pumpkin, beating well between each addition. Stir in chocolate chips and nuts. Divide batter evenly among greased and floured loaf pans. Bake until an inserted tester comes out clean (approximately 45 minutes). Cool. Wrap with plastic wrap and foil. Place in freezer bag. Seal bag, pressing out excess air. Freeze.

Zucchini Bread

(6) 8-inch loaves

9 cups	all-purpose flour
1 tablespoon	salt
1 tablespoon	baking soda

Preheat oven to 350º. In a large mixing bowl, stir together dry ingredients. Set aside.

9	eggs
3 cups	vegetable oil
6 cups	dark brown sugar, packed
6 cups	grated zucchini
3 tablespoons	vanilla
3 cups	walnuts or pecans, chopped

In another large mixing bowl, beat eggs. Add oil, sugar, zucchini, and vanilla. Mix well. Add dry ingredients. Mix well. Fold in nuts. Divide batter evenly among greased and floured loaf pans. Bake until an inserted tester comes out clean (approximately 1 hour). Cool. Wrap with plastic wrap and foil. Place in freezer bag. Seal bag, pressing out excess air. Freeze.

Cookie Dough

Chocolate Chip Cookies
Chocolate Chocolate Chip Cookies with Macadamia Nuts
Molasses Cookies
Oatmeal Cookies with White Chocolate Chips, Dried Cherries & Walnuts
Orange Cranberry Oatmeal Cookies
Oatmeal Date Cookies
Peanut Butter Cookies
Shortbread
Sugar Cookies

Chocolate Chip Cookies

approximately 9 to 10 cups

3½ cups	all-purpose flour
2 teaspoons	salt
1½ teaspoons	baking soda

In a large bowl, combine dry ingredients. Set aside.

1½ cups	vegetable shortening
2½ cups	light brown sugar, packed
¼ cup	milk
2 tablespoons	vanilla
2	eggs

In a large mixing bowl, beat vegetable shortening, brown sugar, milk, and vanilla until creamy. Beat in eggs. Gradually beat or stir in flour mixture.

2 cups	chocolate chips
1 cup	pecans, chopped (optional)
2 tablespoons	orange zest

Stir in chocolate chips, pecans, and orange zest. Portion and freeze in desired packaging.

Baking Instructions

Defrost in refrigerator. Preheat oven to 375°. Drop dough by rounded tablespoon onto ungreased baking sheet. Bake 8 to 10 minutes (chewy cookies) or 11 to 13 minutes (crispy cookies).

Chocolate Chocolate Chip Cookies with Macadamia Nuts

approximately 9 to 10 cups

4 cups	all-purpose flour
1⅓ cups	cocoa powder
4 teaspoons	baking powder
2 teaspoons	baking soda
1 teaspoon	salt

In a large bowl, combine dry ingredients. Set aside.

2 cups	butter, softened
3 cups	sugar
2 teaspoons	vanilla
4	eggs

In a large mixing bowl, beat butter, sugar, and vanilla until creamy. Beat in eggs. Gradually beat or stir in flour mixture.

| 2 cups | chocolate chips (white or semi-sweet) |
| 1½ cups | macadamia nuts, coarsely chopped |

Stir in chocolate chips and macadamia nuts. Portion and freeze in desired packaging.

Baking Instructions

Defrost in refrigerator. Preheat oven to 350°. Drop dough by rounded tablespoon onto ungreased baking sheet. Bake 8 to 10 minutes.

With a varied supply of homemade cookie dough in the freezer, you'll find yourself well prepared for last minute entertaining, after school snacks, or late night cravings for warm cookies, fresh from the oven!

Molasses Cookies

approximately 9 to 10 cups

cups	all-purpose flour
7½ teaspoons	baking soda
1 tablespoon	ground cinnamon
½ teaspoons	ground cloves
1½ teaspoons	ground cardamom
teaspoon	salt

In a large bowl, combine dry ingredients. Set aside.

2¼ cups	vegetable shortening
cups	sugar
cup	molasses
	eggs

In a large mixing bowl, beat vegetable shortening, sugar, and molasses until creamy. Beat in eggs. Gradually beat or stir in flour mixture. Portion and freeze in desired packaging.

Baking Instructions

Defrost in refrigerator. Preheat oven to 350º. Shape dough into 1-inch balls and roll in granulated sugar to coat. Place 2 inches apart onto ungreased baking sheet. Flatten by making crisscross marks with a fork. Bake 8 to 10 minutes.

Oatmeal Cookies with White Chocolate Chips, Dried Cherries & Walnuts

approximately 9 to 10 cups

2½ cups	all-purpose flour
1 teaspoon	baking powder
1 teaspoon	baking soda
1 teaspoon	ground cinnamon
½ teaspoon	salt

In a large bowl, combine dry ingredients. Set aside.

1½ cups	butter, softened
1½ cups	brown sugar, packed
⅔ cup	sugar
1 tablespoon	vanilla
2	eggs
¼ cup	milk

In a large mixing bowl, beat butter, sugars, and vanilla until creamy. Beat in eggs and milk. Gradually beat or stir in flour mixture.

2 cups	quick or old-fashioned oats
2 cups	white chocolate chips
1 cup	dried cherries
1 cup	walnuts, chopped

Stir in oats, white chocolate chips, dried cherries, and nuts. Portion and freeze in desired packaging.

Baking Instructions

Defrost in refrigerator. Preheat oven to 375º. Drop dough by rounded tablespoon onto ungreased baking sheet. Bake 10 to 14 minutes.

Orange Cranberry Oatmeal Cookies

approximately 9 to 10 cups

2 cups	butter, softened
1⅓ cups	sugar
3	large egg yolks
3 tablespoons	orange juice concentrate (from frozen)
1 tablespoon	vanilla
4⅔ cups	all-purpose flour
½ teaspoon	salt

In large mixing bowl, beat together butter, sugar, and vanilla until creamy. Beat in yolks, one at a time, and orange juice concentrate. Gradually beat or stir in flour and salt.

1 cup	walnuts, chopped
1 cup	dried cranberries
1½ cups	quick or old-fashioned oats
1 tablespoon	orange zest

In a small bowl soak cranberries in warm water 15 minutes. Drain cranberries well and chop fine. Stir in walnuts, cranberries, oats, and orange zest. Portion and freeze in desired packaging.

Baking Instructions

Defrost in refrigerator. Preheat oven to 350º. Drop dough by rounded tablespoon onto ungreased baking sheet. Bake 10 to 12 minutes.

Oatmeal Date Cookies

approximately 11 to 12 cups

3 cups	all-purpose flour
2 teaspoons	baking soda
1 teaspoon	ground cinnamon
1 teaspoon	salt

In a large bowl, combine dry ingredients. Set aside.

2 cups	butter, softened
1½ cups	brown sugar, packed
1½ cups	sugar
2 teaspoons	vanilla
4 large	eggs

In a large mixing bowl, beat butter, sugars, and vanilla together until creamy. Beat in eggs. Gradually beat or stir in flour mixture.

6 cups	quick or old-fashioned oats
2 cups	pitted dates, chopped (or raisins)

Stir in oats and dates. Portion and freeze in desired packaging.

Baking Instructions

Defrost in refrigerator. Preheat oven to 350º. Drop dough by rounded tablespoon onto ungreased baking sheet. Bake 10 to 14 minutes.

Peanut Butter Cookies

approximately 9 to 10 cups

¾ cups	all-purpose flour
½ teaspoons	baking powder
½ teaspoons	baking soda

In a large bowl, combine dry ingredients. Set aside.

½ cups	butter, softened
½ cups	peanut butter
½ cups	sugar
½ cups	brown sugar, packed
	eggs
½ teaspoons	vanilla

In a large mixing bowl, beat together butter and peanut butter for 30 seconds. Add sugars and vanilla and beat until creamy. Beat in eggs. Gradually beat or stir in flour. Portion and freeze in desired packaging.

Baking Instructions

Defrost in refrigerator. Preheat oven to 375º. Shape dough into 1-inch balls and roll in granulated sugar to coat. Place onto ungreased baking sheet. Flatten by making crisscross marks with a fork. Bake 7 to 9 minutes.

Shortbread

(6) 8-inch cake pans

1½ cups	sugar
1½ teaspoons	salt
3 cups	butter
1½ teaspoons	vanilla
6 cups	flour

Work in batches as necessary. In a large bowl, stir sugar and salt together. Process or cut in butter until smooth. Blend in vanilla. Add flour and process or cut in until crumbly, scraping down sides of bowl. Divide between 6 8-inch cake pans. Using a piece of plastic wrap, press dough firmly and evenly. Wrap with plastic wrap and foil. Place in freezer bag. Seal bag, pressing out excess air. Freeze.

Baking Instructions

Defrost in refrigerator. While chilled, place in 300° preheated oven. Bake until pale gold in color (approximately 45 minutes). While warm, cut into wedges. Cool completely.

Modify shortbread by adding or substituting your favorite flavors. Almond extract may be substituted for vanilla. Consider adding orange zest, lemon zest, or mini morsels. Or press your favorite chopped nuts into the top of the shortbread before freezing.

Sugar Cookies

approximately 8 cups

6 cups	**flour**
1½ teaspoons	**baking powder**
¾ teaspoon	**salt**

In a large bowl, combine dry ingredients. Set aside.

1½ cups	**butter, softened**
3 cups	**sugar**
3	**eggs**
1 tablespoon	**vanilla**

In a large mixing bowl, beat butter, sugar, and vanilla until creamy. Beat in eggs. Gradually beat or stir in flour mixture. Portion and form into ready-to-roll flattened disks. Wrap in plastic wrap and in foil. Freeze.

Baking Instructions

Defrost in refrigerator. Preheat oven to 325°. Roll chilled dough to ⅛-inch. Cut into desired shapes. Place cookies on ungreased baking sheet and refrigerate 10 minutes. Bake until edges begin to brown (approximately 8 to 10 minutes).

Children love to roll, cut, and decorate cookies. Freezing dough ahead of time gives them a shortcut to fun!

Desserts

Apple Crisp
Brownies with Chocolate Buttercream Frosting
Cheesecake
Layered Chocolate Nut Bars
Coconut Cake with Coconut Cream Frosting
Lemon Bars
Magic Layer Bars
Peach Streusel Pie
Pound Cake
Pumpkin Ice Cream Pie
Vanilla Ice Cream Cake with Chocolate Sauce

Apple Crisp

(6) 5" x 7" or

(3) 5" x 12" or 8" x 8" or

(2) 9" x 13"

6 pounds	apples, peeled, cored, and sliced
1 tablespoon	lemon juice
½ cup	brown sugar, packed

In a large bowl, mix together apples, lemon juice, and brown sugar. Divide apples evenly among tins.

1½ cups	brown sugar, packed
1½ cups	all-purpose flour
1 cup	quick or old-fashioned oats
¾ cup	butter, softened

In a large mixing bowl, mix together sugar, flour, oats, and butter. Divide evenly among tins, sprinkling over sliced apples. Cover with a sheet of plastic, pressing down to cling to food. Apply board lid. Freeze.

Baking Instructions

Defrost completely. Remove board lid and plastic wrap. Preheat oven to 375°. Bake until apples are tender (approximately 45 minutes).

Brownies with Chocolate Buttercream Frosting

(6) 5" x 7" or

(3) 5" x 12" or 8" x 8" or

(2) 9" x 13"

8 ounces	unsweetened chocolate
1 cup	butter
1½ tablespoons	instant coffee granules

In a heavy saucepan over low heat, melt chocolate and butter. Whisk in coffee granules. Remove from heat. Cool.

8	eggs
1 teaspoon	salt
3 cups	sugar
¾ cup	liqueur (Godiva or Kahlua)
2 teaspoons	vanilla
¾ cup	all-purpose flour, sifted
2 cups	walnuts, chopped

Preheat oven to 450°. In a large mixing bowl, beat together eggs and salt. Gradually add sugar and beat until ribbony (approximately 8 minutes). While beating on low speed, add liqueur, vanilla, and cooled chocolate mixture. Fold in flour. Fold in nuts. Divide batter evenly among tins. Upon placing brownies in oven, lower temperature to 400°. Bake until tester inserted into center comes out clean (approximately 20 minutes). Cool.

Chocolate Buttercream Frosting

1 cup	butter, softened
2 cups	powdered sugar, sifted
1 cup	cocoa powder, sifted
⅓ cup	liqueur (Godiva or Kahlua)

In a large mixing bowl, cream butter until smooth. Sift powdered sugar and cocoa powder over butter. Add liqueur and beat until smooth. Frost brownies. Cover with sheet of plastic wrap, pressing down to cling to food. Apply board lid. Freeze.

Cheesecake

(2) 8-inch cheesecakes

cups	graham cracker crumbs
tablespoons	butter, melted
cup	sugar

reheat oven to 375°. In a mixing bowl, mix graham cracker crumbs, melted butter, nd sugar until thoroughly combined. Divide evenly among pie tins. Press crumbs rmly into bottoms, and up sides, of tins. Bake 5 minutes. Cool completely. Set ide.

pounds	cream cheese, softened
⅓ cup	sugar
cup	milk
cup	all-purpose flour
teaspoons	vanilla
teaspoon	salt
	large eggs

reheat oven to 325°. Work in batches as necessary. In a food processor, process cream heese, sugar, milk, flour, vanilla, and salt until smooth. Add eggs, one at a time, pro- essing after each addition. Divide evenly among crusts. Bake 1 hour. Cool com- letely. Cover with plastic wrap and foil. Place in freezer bag. Seal bag, pressing out xcess air. Freeze.

> Cheesecakes freeze beautifully! We've chosen to include a plain cheesecake recipe, knowing it can be trans- formed upon serving. Add seasonal fruits, decadent sauces, chopped nuts, and/or whipped cream.

Layered Chocolate Nut Bars

(6) 5" x 7" or

(3) 5" x 12" or 8" x 8" or

(2) 9" x 13"

3 cups	flour
1⅓ cups	sugar
1 teaspoon	salt
1½ cups	butter, chilled
2	eggs, lightly beaten

Preheat oven to 350°. In a food processor or mixing bowl, blend together flour, sugar, and salt. Cut in butter. Add egg and blend until dough forms. Divide evenly among tins. Using a piece of plastic wrap, press dough evenly and firmly into bottom of tins. Remove plastic wrap. Bake until lightly browned (approximately 20 minutes). Remove from oven and maintain oven temperature.

1 cup	butter, softened
2 cups	brown sugar, packed
4	eggs
½ cup	flour
1 tablespoon	vanilla
1 teaspoon	salt
6 cups	pecans, chopped
4 cups	chocolate morsels

In a large mixing bowl, cream butter and brown sugar. Add eggs, one at a time, and beat well after each addition. Add flour, vanilla, and salt. Blend well. Stir in pecans and chocolate morsels. Divide and spread filling over baked crusts. Return to oven and bake until browned (approximately 25 minutes). Cool completely. Cover with a sheet of plastic wrap, pressing down to cling to food. Apply board lid. Freeze.

Coconut Cake with Coconut Cream Frosting

(6) 5" x 7" or

(3) 5" x 12" or 8" x 8" or

(2) 9" x 13"

30 ounces	**canned cream of coconut (Coco Lopez), shaken**

Reserve 1 cup cream of coconut for use in frosting.

8	**eggs, separated**

In a large mixing bowl, whip egg whites until stiff but not dry. Reserve yolks. Set aside.

5½ cups	**all-purpose flour**
2 teaspoons	**baking powder**
1 teaspoon	**baking soda**
1 teaspoon	**salt**

In a large mixing bowl, stir together dry ingredients. Set aside.

3½ cups	**sugar**
2 cups	**butter, softened**
1 tablespoon	**vanilla**
2 cups	**buttermilk**

Preheat oven to 350°. In a large mixing bowl, cream sugar, butter, and unreserved cream of coconut. Beat in egg yolks and vanilla. Beat in dry ingredients. Beat in buttermilk until just blended. Fold beaten egg whites into batter. Divide batter evenly among tins. Bake until tester inserted into center comes out clean (approximately 45 minutes). Cool. Maintain oven temperature.

Coconut Cream Frosting

3 cups	**shredded coconut**

Work in batches as necessary. Spread shredded coconut on a foil-lined baking tray. Place in oven and toast 5 minutes. Stir. Toast 2 to 3 more minutes. Stir. Repeat as necessary until coconut is adequately toasted. Set aside.

2 pounds	**cream cheese, softened**
1 cup	**butter, softened**
1 cup	**reserved canned cream of coconut**
5 cups	**powdered sugar**
1 tablespoon	**vanilla**

In a food processor or mixing bowl, process or beat cream cheese, butter and reserved cream of coconut until smooth. Add powdered sugar and vanilla. Process or beat until smooth. Divide and spread frosting evenly among cakes. Divide toasted coconut among cakes and sprinkle. Cover with plastic wrap and foil. Place in a freezer bag. Seal bag, pressing out excess air. Freeze.

Lemon Bars

(6) 5" x 7" or

(3) 5" x 12" or 8" x 8" or

(2) 9" x 13"

3 cups	all-purpose flour
1 cup	powdered sugar
1½ cups	butter

Preheat oven to 350°. In a food processor or mixing bowl, combine flour and powdered sugar. Cut in butter. Divide evenly among tins. Using a piece of plastic wrap, press dough evenly and firmly into bottom of tins. Remove plastic wrap. Bake until lightly browned (approximately 15 to 20 minutes). Remove from oven and maintain oven temperature.

8	eggs
2½ cups	sugar
1 cup	fresh lemon juice
3 tablespoons	all-purpose flour
2 tablespoons	lemon zest

In a large mixing bowl, beat eggs together with sugar, lemon juice, flour, and lemon zest. Divide and pour filling over baked crusts. Bake until mixture is set (approximately 15 to 20 minutes). Remove from oven. Dust with powdered sugar. Cool. Cover with a sheet of plastic wrap. Apply board lid. Freeze.

P op cakes, brownies and bars out of packaging materials while still frozen. For beautiful clean cuts, cut while partially frozen. Dust powdered sugar-topped items a second time before serving.

Magic Layer Bars

(6) 5" x 7" or

(3) 5" x 12" or 8" x 8" or

(2) 9" x 13"

| 1 cup | butter, softened |
| 3 cups | graham cracker crumbs |

Preheat oven to 350°. Divide butter evenly among tins. Place in oven just until butter melts. Divide graham cracker crumbs and sprinkle evenly among tins.

28 ounces	canned sweetened condensed milk
2 cups	chocolate morsels
2⅔ cups	shredded coconut
2 cups	nuts, chopped

Pour sweetened condensed milk over graham cracker crumbs, dividing evenly among tins. Top evenly with remaining ingredients. Press down morsels, coconut, and nuts. Bake until lightly browned (approximately 20 to 30 minutes). Cool. Cover with plastic wrap, pressing down to cling to food. Apply board lid. Freeze.

V ary this crowd pleaser by substituting different flavored morsels!

Peach Streusel Pie

(3) 9-inch pies

Pie Crust

3 cups	all-purpose flour
¼ teaspoon	baking powder
¼ teaspoon	salt
1 cup	vegetable shortening
½ cup	butter, chilled
½ cup	ice water

In a food processor or mixing bowl, mix together all dry ingredients. Cut in vegetable shortening and butter. Add ice water a little at a time, processing until dough forms. Divide into 3 equal portions. Form into disks, wrap in plastic wrap, and chill 30 minutes. Roll, press into pie tin, and crimp edges. Place in refrigerator or freezer.

Streusel Topping

3 cups	all-purpose flour
2 cups	brown sugar, firmly packed
1½ cups	quick or old-fashioned oats
1 teaspoon	cinnamon
1¼ cups	butter, melted

In a mixing bowl, stir together all dry ingredients. Add melted butter and stir until moist clumps form. Set aside.

Peach Filling

6 to 7 pounds	fresh peaches, peeled and sliced
¼ cup	fresh lemon juice
¾ teaspoon	pure almond extract
2¼ cups	sugar
½ cup	quick-cooking tapioca
1½ teaspoons	ascorbic acid (Fruit Fresh)
¾ teaspoon	salt

In a large bowl, gently toss peach slices with lemon juice and almond extract. Combine sugar, tapioca, ascorbic acid, and salt. Stir thoroughly. Pour over peaches and stir to combine. Divide filling evenly among pie shells. Divide streusel topping evenly among tins. Cover with plastic wrap. Freeze overnight. Once frozen, wrap entire pie in foil and place in a freezer bag. Seal bag, pressing out excess air. Return to freezer.

Baking Instructions

Preheat oven to 425°. Bake frozen pie 45 minutes. Reduce oven temperature to 350°. Cover loosely with foil to halt browning if necessary. Continue baking until bubbly (approximately 30 more minutes).

Vary pie fillings to include your favorite fruits. We like to use a streusel or crisp topping because it cuts pastry rolling efforts in half! Double the pie crust ingredients if your preference is a double crust pie.

Pound Cake

(6) 8-inch loaves or

(2) bundt cakes

6 cups	all-purpose flour
½ teaspoon	baking powder

Preheat oven to 300°. In a mixing bowl, stir together flour and baking powder. Set aside.

2 cups	butter, softened
6 cups	sugar
12	eggs
2 cups	sour cream
2 teaspoons	almond extract
2 teaspoons	vanilla

In a large mixing bowl, cream butter and sugar. Add eggs, two at a time, and beat well after each addition. Beginning and ending with dry mixture, add alternating with sour cream, beating well between each addition. Blend in almond and vanilla extracts. Divide batter evenly among tins. Bake 1 to 1¼ hours, or until cake pulls away from the side of the tin. Cool in tin 10 minutes. Remove from tin and invert on rack to cool completely. Return to tins. Cover with plastic wrap, pressing down to cling to cake. Wrap in foil and place in a freezer bag. Seal bag, pressing out excess air. Freeze.

Pound cake is a versatile frozen food item! Flavor the batter with orange or lemon zest, mini morsels, or finely chopped nuts. Serve with your favorite sauces, ice creams, or fresh fruits.

Pumpkin Ice Cream Pie

(3) 9-inch pies

3 cups	graham cracker crumbs
9 tablespoons	butter, melted
6 tablespoons	sugar

Preheat oven to 375°. In a mixing bowl, mix graham cracker crumbs, melted butter, and sugar until thoroughly combined. Divide evenly among pie tins. Press crumbs firmly into bottoms, and up sides, of tins. Bake 5 minutes. Cool completely. Set aside.

3 pints	vanilla ice cream, softened

Spoon ice cream into pie shells. Freeze until firm.

3 cups	pumpkin purée
3 cups	sugar
1½ teaspoons	ground ginger
1½ teaspoons	ground cinnamon
¾ teaspoon	ground nutmeg
¾ teaspoon	salt
3 cups	whipping cream

In a mixing bowl, combine pumpkin, sugar, ginger, cinnamon, nutmeg, and salt. Stir to evenly combine. In a second mixing bowl, beat whipping cream until stiff. Fold into pumpkin mixture. Divide evenly between pie shells, mounding on top of frozen ice cream layer. Cover with plastic wrap. Freeze overnight. Once frozen, wrap in foil and place in a freezer bag. Seal bag, pressing out excess air. Return to freezer.

Serving Instructions

Defrost at least 15 minutes before cutting. Serve with caramel sauce, if desired.

Vanilla Ice Cream Cake
with Chocolate Sauce

(6) 5" x 7" or

(3) 5" x 12" or 8" x 8" or

(2) 9" x 13"

Crust

72	**chocolate wafer cookies**
1½ cups	**butter, melted**

Preheat oven to 325°. Work in batches as necessary. In a mixing bowl or processor, process chocolate wafers into fine crumbs. Add melted butter and process until combined. Divide evenly among pie tins. Press crumbs firmly into bottoms, and up sides, of tins. Bake until set (approximately 10 to 12 minutes). Cool completely. Set aside.

Chocolate Sauce

3 cups	**heavy cream**
½ cup	**butter**
½ cup	**light corn syrup**
2 pounds	**bittersweet (not unsweetened) or semisweet chocolate, chopped**

In a medium saucepan over medium heat, combine cream, butter, and corn syrup. Bring to simmer. Remove from heat. Add bittersweet chocolate and let stand 1 minute. Whisk until melted and smooth. Let stand at room temperature until cool and slightly thickened (approximately 20 minutes).

18 cups	**vanilla ice cream, softened**
6	**Heath bars, crushed**

Divide and spread half of vanilla ice cream evenly among tins. Divide and drizzle half of chocolate sauce evenly among tins. Divide and spread remaining half of vanilla ice cream evenly among tins. Divide and spread remaining half of chocolate sauce evenly among tins. Divide and sprinkle crushed Heath bar pieces evenly among tins. Cover with plastic wrap. Freeze overnight. Once frozen, wrap entire cake in foil and place in a freezer bag. Seal bag, pressing out excess air. Return to freezer.

Serving Instructions

Defrost at least 15 minutes before cutting.

Ice cream pies and cakes are wonderful do-ahead desserts for entertaining. They're pleasing to young and old and the possibilities of flavors and combinations are endless!

Soup's On

Austrian Steak Soup
Chicken and White Bean Soup
Chicken with Wild Rice Soup
French Onion Soup
Hearty Turkey Noodle Soup
Lentil Soup
Puréed Winter Squash Soup

Austrian Steak Soup

approximately 36 cups

	olive or vegetable oil
6 pounds	beef, cut into small pieces
	salt and pepper to taste

Work in batches as necessary. In a large skillet or Dutch oven over medium-high heat, heat oil. Season and brown beef chunks. Refrigerate. Reserve meat juices and reduce to taste.

3	onions, chopped
3	celery ribs, chopped
1 tablespoon	garlic, pressed or minced
½ cup	all-purpose flour
½ cup	sweet Hungarian paprika
16 cups	beef stock or canned broth
6 cups	water
6	bay leaves
½ cup	tomato paste
2 teaspoons	salt
½ cup	apple cider vinegar
1½ tablespoons	dried thyme

Work in batches as necessary. In a large stockpot over medium heat, heat oil. Sauté onions, celery, and garlic until softened. Stir in flour and paprika and cook 3 minutes. Stir in beef stock or canned broth, water, bay leaves, tomato paste, salt, vinegar, and thyme. Add cooked beef and simmer, stirring occasionally, until meat is tender (approximately 1 hour).

| 1½ pounds | carrots, sliced |
| 8 | potatoes, peeled and cubed |

Add carrots and simmer 10 minutes. Add potatoes and simmer 15 more minutes (potatoes should be slightly undercooked). Remove from heat. Remove and discard bay leaves. Cool. Divide evenly among among freezer bags. Seal bag, pressing out excess air. Freeze.

Reheating Instructions

Defrost in refrigerator. Transfer to saucepan or microwave safe dish and heat thoroughly.

Chicken and White Bean Soup

approximately 36 cups

| | olive or vegetable oil |
| 4 pounds | boneless, skinless chicken breasts, cut into bite-sized pieces |

Work in batches as necessary. In a large skillet over medium-high heat, heat oil. Add chicken to skillet and sauté, stirring occasionally, until cooked through. Transfer chicken to large bowl, removing batches from skillet with a slotted spoon. Refrigerate. Discard juices.

	olive or vegetable oil
4	medium onions, chopped
1 pound	carrots, diced
2 tablespoons	garlic, pressed or minced
16 cups	chicken stock or canned broth
32 ounces	canned diced tomatoes, undrained
2 cups	water
24 ounces	frozen green beans
45 ounces	canned white beans, rinsed and drained
20 ounces	frozen chopped spinach, thawed and drained
1 tablespoon	dried basil
	salt and pepper to taste

Work in batches as necessary. In a large stockpot over medium-high heat, heat oil. Sauté onions, carrots, and garlic until tender. Stir in chicken stock or canned broth, tomatoes, frozen green beans, and water. Bring to a boil. Reduce heat and simmer, uncovered, until beans are tender (approximately 10 minutes). Stir in canned white beans, chicken, drained spinach, and basil until heated through. Remove from heat. Season with salt and pepper. Cool. Divide evenly among freezer bags. Seal bag, pressing out excess air. Freeze.

Reheating Instructions

Defrost in refrigerator. Transfer to saucepan or microwave safe dish and heat thoroughly.

Chicken with Wild Rice Soup

approximately 36 cups

pounds	boneless, skinless chicken breasts, cut into bite-sized pieces

Work in batches as necessary. In a large skillet over medium-high heat, heat oil. Add chicken to skillet and sauté, stirring occasionally, until cooked through. Transfer chicken to large bowl, removing batches from skillet with a slotted spoon. Refrigerate. Discard juices.

cups	wild rice, washed
pound	long-grain white rice

Prepare rice according to package directions. Set aside.

	olive or vegetable oil
	medium onions, chopped
pound	carrots, diced
	celery ribs, diced
tablespoons	garlic, pressed or minced
cup	all-purpose flour
½ teaspoons	dried tarragon
½ teaspoons	dried thyme
cup	dry sherry
2 cups	chicken stock or canned broth
cups	canned evaporated milk
	salt and pepper to taste

Work in batches as necessary. In a large stockpot over medium-high heat, heat oil. Sauté onions, carrots, celery, and garlic until onions are tender. Add flour, tarragon, and thyme and cook 3 to 5 minutes, stirring constantly. Stir in sherry, chicken stock or canned broth, and evaporated milk. Bring to a boil. Reduce heat and simmer, uncovered, until lightly thickened (approximately 20 to 25 minutes). Remove from heat and transfer to a large container for combining ingredients. Stir in cooked rice and chicken. Cool. Divide evenly among freezer bags. Seal bag, pressing out excess air. Freeze.

Reheating Instructions

Defrost in refrigerator. Transfer to saucepan or microwave safe dish and gently simmer over low heat.

French Onion Soup

approximately 32 cups

1 cup	butter
9 pounds	onions, thinly sliced
¼ cup	garlic, pressed or minced
1½ cups	dry white wine
¼ cup	all-purpose flour
10 cups	chicken stock or canned broth
13 cups	beef stock or canned broth
1 tablespoon	Dijon mustard
	salt and pepper to taste

Work in batches as necessary. In a large stockpot over medium-high heat, heat oil. Sauté onions and garlic until tender and brown (approximately 30 to 40 minutes). Add wine and simmer until reduced. Stir in flour and cook 1 minute. Add stocks or canned broths and mustard. Bring to a boil. Reduce heat and simmer, uncovered, 20 minutes. Remove from heat. Season with salt and pepper. Cool. Divide evenly among freezer bags. Seal bag, pressing out excess air.

24 slices	French baguette cut into 1-inch slices
24 slices	mozzarella or Swiss cheese

Package bread in snack bags (1 slice per serving). Package cheese in snack bags (1 slice per serving). Attach a package of bread and a package of cheese to each container of soup. Freeze.

Reheating Instructions

Defrost in refrigerator. Reheat soup. Ladle hot soup into broiler safe bowls. Toast bread and top each bowl with a slice of toast and a slice of cheese. Broil until cheese melts and bubbles.

Hearty Turkey Noodle Soup

approximately 36 cups

2	4 to 5 pound turkey breasts

Roast turkey breasts. See *Preparing Turkey*. Cool. Debone and cut turkey into bite-sized chunks. Refrigerate. Reserve stock and reduce to taste.

½ cup	butter
4	medium onions, chopped
1 pound	carrots, diced
8	celery ribs, diced
32 cups	turkey stock or canned chicken broth (include reserved stock)
1 pound	homemade style egg noodles
½ cup	dried parsley
	salt and pepper to taste

Work in batches as necessary. In a large stockpot over medium-high heat, melt butter. Sauté onions, carrots, and celery until onions are tender. Add turkey stock and chicken broth. Bring to a boil. Stir in egg noodles, parsley, and chunked turkey. Lower heat and simmer 30 minutes, stirring occasionally. Remove from heat. Season with salt and pepper. Cool. Divide evenly among freezer bags. Seal bag, pressing out excess air. Freeze.

Reheating Instructions

Defrost in refrigerator. Transfer to saucepan or microwave safe dish and heat thoroughly.

For a therapeutic chicken noodle soup, substitute 10 cups cooked, chunked chicken for turkey.

Lentil Soup

approximately 36 cups

84 ounces	canned diced tomatoes, undrained
½ cup	butter
4	medium onions, chopped
1 pound	carrots, diced
16	celery ribs, diced
14 cups	chicken stock or canned broth
2 cups	dried lentils
1 cup	dry red wine (Burgundy or Cabernet)
½ cup	dried parsley
4 teaspoons	garlic, pressed or minced
	salt and pepper to taste

Work in batches as necessary. Purée tomatoes in blender. Set aside. In a large stockpot over medium-high heat, melt butter. Sauté onions, carrots, and celery until onions are tender. Add tomatoes, chicken stock or canned broth, and lentils. Bring to a boil. Lower heat and simmer 30 minutes, stirring occasionally. Add wine, parsley, and garlic. Simmer 30 more minutes, stirring occasionally. Remove from heat. Season with salt and pepper. Cool. Divide evenly among freezer bags. Seal bag, pressing out excess air. Freeze.

Reheating Instructions

Defrost in refrigerator. Transfer to saucepan or microwave safe dish and heat thoroughly.

Puréed Winter Squash Soup

approximately 36 cups

	acorn squash (about 8 pounds total)
to 3	butternut squash (about 8 pounds total)
cup	butter
cup	brown sugar
	salt

eheat oven to 350°. Cut squash in half, discarding seeds. Place on baking sheets, in side down. In the cavity of each squash half, place 1 tablespoon butter and 1 tea-oon brown sugar. Season with salt. Roast until tender (approximately 1 hour). ool.

pound	carrots, peeled and cut into thirds
	large onions, sliced
cup	olive oil
	salt and pepper

ace carrots and onion slices on baking sheet. Drizzle with olive oil. Toss to coat. ason with salt and pepper. Roast until tender and brown (approximately 45 minutes).

2 cups	chicken stock or canned broth
teaspoons	ground ginger
teaspoon	cinnamon
teaspoon	ground mace
	salt and pepper

oop squash pulp from skins and place in large stockpot. Add roasted carrots and ions. Stir in chicken stock or canned broth, ginger, cinnamon, and mace. Bring to oil. Reduce heat and simmer, uncovered, 20 minutes. Remove from heat. Season with salt and pepper. Cool. Puree in batches. Transfer to a large bowl and stir thor-oughly to harmonize batches. Divide evenly among freezer bags. Seal bag, pressing out excess air. Freeze.

Reheating Instructions

Defrost in refrigerator. Transfer to saucepan or microwave safe dish and heat thoroughly.

This is a delicious, creamy soup . . . without the cream! Consider it a great way to freeze plentiful and economi-cal fall squash.

Party Foods

Artichoke Squares
Feta Phyllo Triangles
Guacamole
Hummus
Mexican Bean Dip
Pesto Spread with Pine Nuts
Mushroom Turnovers
Sun Dried Tomato Spread
Three Cheese Ball

Artichoke Squares

(6) 5" x 7" or

(3) 5" x 12" or 8" x 8" or

(2) 9" x 13"

	olive or vegetable oil
36 ounces	artichoke hearts, drained and chopped
3	small onions, finely chopped
¾ cup	plain breadcrumbs
½ teaspoon	ground black pepper
½ teaspoon	dried oregano
½ teaspoon	Tabasco sauce
6 cups	shredded cheddar cheese
¼ cup	dried parsley
1 teaspoon	salt
12	eggs

Preheat oven to 325°. In a skillet over medium heat, heat oil. Sauté onions until tender and remove from heat. In a large bowl, beat eggs. Stir in remaining ingredients, including sautéed onion. Divide evenly among tins. Bake 30 minutes. Cool. Cover with a sheet of plastic wrap, pressing down to cling to food. Apply board lid. Freeze.

Serving Instructions

Defrost in refrigerator. Preheat oven to 350°. Remove board lid and plastic wrap. Bake until heated through (approximately 20 minutes).

Feta Phyllo Triangles

50 to 60 pieces

2	eggs
8 ounces	feta cheese
8 ounces	cream cheese, softened
¼ cup	fresh spinach or fresh parsley
¼ cup	green onion, finely chopped
1 teaspoon	dried mint

In a blender or food processor, blend eggs and cheeses. Add spinach or parsley, green onion, and mint. Chop. Refrigerate until ready to fill triangles.

1	one pound package phyllo dough
1½ cups	butter, melted

Defrost phyllo dough overnight in refrigerator. Mist a clean kitchen towel with water. Remove phyllo sheets from box; open flat and cover with towel. Remove one sheet. Brush with melted butter. Top with a second sheet. Brush with melted butter. Using a pizza cutter, cut sheet into six strips (lengthwise). Place 1 rounded teaspoon filling at the end of each strip. Fold corner over filling to form a triangle. Continue folding, back and forth, maintaining triangular shape. Place on foil-lined baking sheet. Brush with melted butter. Continue until all phyllo sheets have been used. Freeze overnight. Portion and place in freezer bags. Seal bags, pressing out excess air. Return to freezer.

Baking Instructions

Preheat oven to 375°. Place frozen triangles on an ungreased baking sheet. Bake until golden (approximately 20 minutes).

Guacamole

approximately 10 cups

¾ cup	fresh lemon juice

Juice lemons. Set aside.

1½ cups	onion, finely chopped
12	ripe avocados
1 tablespoon	garlic, pressed or minced
1 teaspoon	Tabasco sauce, or to taste

Work in batches as necessary. In a food processor, process onion. Halve, seed, and peel avocados. Add avocados, garlic, Tabasco sauce, and fresh lemon juice to processor. Process to desired consistency. Divide evenly among tins, quickly pressing a piece of plastic wrap directly onto the surface to prevent browning. Apply board lid. Freeze.

Serving Instructions

Defrost in refrigerator. Add one seeded, chopped fresh tomato before serving.

Hummus

approximately 12 cups

72 ounces	chickpeas, rinsed and drained
1½ cups	Tahini
1½ cups	fresh lemon juice
1½ cups	olive oil
3 tablespoons	garlic, pressed or minced
¾ to 1½ cups	water
	salt and pepper to taste

Work in batches as necessary. Place chickpeas, Tahini, lemon juice, olive oil, and garlic in processor. Blend until smooth. Add water and process until desired consistency is achieved. Season with salt and pepper. Divide between tins. Cover with a sheet of plastic wrap, pressing down to cling to food. Apply board lid. Freeze.

Serving Instructions

Defrost in refrigerator. Spread hummus on serving platter. Drizzle with olive oil. Serve with warmed pita wedges or raw vegetables.

Appetizers in the freezer are a party waiting to happen. Pop some great crackers and tortilla chips in the pantry to compliment your stash in the freezer!

Mexican Bean Dip

(6) 5" x 7" or

(3) 5" x 12" or 8" x 8" or

(2) 9" x 13"

1½ pounds	cream cheese, softened
48 ounces	canned refried beans
3 cups	sour cream
1½ cups	finely chopped green onion, whites and light stems only
1½ teaspoons	Tabasco sauce (or to taste)
3 tablespoons	chili powder
5 teaspoons	garlic salt
1 tablespoon	onion powder
1½ teaspoons	ground cumin
1½ teaspoons	dried oregano

Work in batches as necessary. In a large mixing bowl or food processor, combine all ingredients. Blend until smooth.

1½ cups	shredded cheddar cheese
1½ cups	shredded Monterey Jack cheese

Divide and spread half of bean dip evenly among tins. Divide and spread half of cheese evenly among tins. Repeat. Cover with a sheet of plastic wrap, pressing down to cling to food. Apply board lid. Freeze.

Baking Instructions

Defrost in refrigerator. Preheat oven to 350°. Remove board lid and plastic wrap. Bake until bubbly (approximately 25 minutes). Serve with tortilla chips or raw vegetables.

Pesto Spread with Pine Nuts

(6) 5" x 7" or

(3) 5" x 12" or 8" x 8" or

(2) 9" x 13"

6 tablespoons	butter, melted
¾ cup	cracker crumbs

Divide melted butter and cracker crumbs evenly among tins. Shake to spread evenly.

¾ cup	pine nuts
1½ pounds	cream cheese, softened
4	eggs
½ cup	heavy cream
¼ cup	butter, melted
4 cups	shredded Parmesan cheese
¾ cup	prepared pesto

Work in batches as necessary. Preheat oven to 325°. Divide pine nuts evenly among snack bags. In a food processor or mixing bowl, process or beat cream cheese until smooth. Add eggs, one at a time. Add cream and butter, beating until smooth. Fold in Parmesan cheese. Divide half of cream cheese mixture evenly among tins. Divide and spread half of pesto evenly among tins. Repeat. Swirl until lightly blended. Bake until puffed and golden (approximately 40 minutes). Cool. Cover with a sheet of plastic wrap, pressing down to cling to food. Place a bag of pine nuts in each tin. Apply board lid. Freeze.

Serving Instructions

While frozen, remove spread from tin. Defrost. Toast pine nuts. Place spread on a serving platter, drizzle with extra virgin olive oil and top with pine nuts. Serve with crackers or toasts.

Mushroom Turnovers

50 to 60 pieces

Filling

3 tablespoons	butter
1	large onion, finely chopped
8 ounces	mushrooms, finely chopped
½ teaspoon	salt
½ teaspoon	pepper
¼ teaspoon	dried thyme
2 tablespoons	all-purpose flour
½ cup	sour cream

In a large skillet over medium heat, melt butter. Add onions and brown. Add mushrooms and cook, stirring frequently, approximately 5 minutes. Stir in seasonings and flour. Add sour cream and stir until thickened. Remove from heat. Cool.

Pastry

12 ounces	cream cheese, softened
¾ cup	butter, softened
2 cups	flour
½ teaspoon	salt

In a large mixing bowl, thoroughly blend cream cheese and butter. Add flour and salt and cut in until smooth. Form into two disks, wrap in plastic wrap and chill 30 minutes. On a lightly floured surface, roll dough to ⅛-inch thickness. Using a cutter or drinking glass, cut into 3-inch rounds. Continue rolling and cutting scraps. In the center of each round, place 1 teaspoon mushroom filling. Fold. Press edges together with a crimper or a fork. Place on a foil-lined cookie sheet. Freeze overnight. Portion and place in freezer bags. Seal bags, pressing out excess air. Return to freezer.

Baking Instructions

Preheat oven to 450°. Place frozen turnovers on a greased baking sheet. Brush with egg wash if desired (1 egg beaten with 1 tablespoon milk). Bake until lightly browned (approximately 10 to 12 minutes).

This cream cheese pastry rolls and cuts beautifully. Try this pastry with any of your favorite fillings!

Sun Dried Tomato Spread

approximately 10 cups

2 pounds	cream cheese, softened
2 pounds	feta cheese, crumbled
2 cups	plain nonfat yogurt
1½ cups	oil-packed sun-dried tomatoes, drained and chopped
¾ cup	pine nuts, toasted
3 tablespoons	dried basil
1 tablespoon	garlic, pressed or minced

Work in batches as necessary. In a large mixing bowl or food processor, combine cream cheese, feta cheese, and yogurt. Blend. Add remaining ingredients and blend/chop. Divide evenly among tins. Cover with a sheet of plastic wrap, pressing down to cling to food. Apply board lid. Freeze.

Serving Instructions

Defrost in refrigerator. Place in a decorative bowl. Serve with crackers or toasts.

Three Cheese Ball

approximately 9 cups

4½ pounds	cream cheese, softened
2¼ cups	shredded Parmesan cheese
2¼ cups	shredded cheddar cheese
1 cup plus 2 tablespoons	sour cream
7 tablespoons	Worcestershire sauce
7 tablespoons	fresh chives, chopped
3 tablespoons	garlic powder
3 cups	nuts of choice, finely chopped

Work in batches as necessary. In a large mixing bowl or food processor, combine all ingredients except nuts. Process until evenly combined. Divide into 6 equal pieces, forming each into a ball. Roll in chopped nuts. Wrap in plastic wrap and foil. Freeze.

Serving Instructions

Defrost in refrigerator. Place on platter and serve with crackers.

Breakfast

Baked French Toast
Blueberry Coffee Cake
Buttermilk Waffles
Granola
Morning Glory Muffins
Oven Omelet
Potato Sausage Bake
Scrambled Egg and Cheese Biscuits

Baked French Toast

16 slices

1 pound	French bread cut into 16 slices
8	eggs
2 cups	milk
1 cup	heavy cream
2 teaspoons	vanilla
½ teaspoon	cinnamon

Spray a tin with nonstick cooking spray. Arrange bread slices in the bottom of each tin. In a large bowl, beat together eggs, milk, cream, vanilla, and cinnamon. Pour over bread slices, dividing evenly among tins. Cover and refrigerate at least 8 hours or overnight.

¾ cup	butter
1¼ cups	brown sugar, packed
3 tablespoons	light corn syrup

Preheat oven to 350°. In a small saucepan over medium heat, combine butter, brown sugar, and corn syrup. Bring to a boil, stirring constantly. Remove from stovetop and pour over bread and egg mixture, dividing evenly among tins. Bake, uncovered, 40 minutes. Cool completely. Cover with a sheet of plastic, pressing down to cling to food. Apply foil lid. Freeze.

Reheating Instructions

Defrost in refrigerator. Preheat oven to 350°. Remove board lid and plastic wrap. Cover loosely with foil. Bake until heated through (approximately 15 to 20 minutes). Sprinkle with powdered sugar and toasted pecans if desired.

Blueberry Coffee Cake

(6) 5" x 7" or
(3) 5" x 12" or 8" x 8" or
(2) 9" x 13"

4 cups	all-purpose flour
3 cups	sugar
1⅛ cups	butter, room temperature

Preheat oven to 350º. In a large mixing bowl, stir together flour and sugar. Add butter and cut in with a pastry knife. Reserve 1½ cups of this mixture for crumb topping. Set aside.

2 cups	milk
4	eggs
4 teaspoons	baking powder
3 cups	blueberries, fresh or frozen

Add milk, eggs, and baking powder to flour mixture. Beat at moderate speed until smooth (approximately 3 minutes). Divide batter evenly among tins. Top batter with blueberries, dividing evenly among tins. Divide and sprinkle crumb topping evenly among tins. Bake until an inserted tester comes out clean (approximately 40 minutes). Cool. Cover with a sheet of plastic wrap, pressing down to cling to food. Apply foil lid. Freeze.

A coffee cake in the freezer is a terrific asset! It performs marvelously as a dessert, breakfast item, brunch item or snack. Consider freezing in individually-sized portions for snacks-on-the-go!

Buttermilk Waffles

12 to 16 waffles

cups	all-purpose flour
tablespoons	sugar
tablespoon	baking powder
teaspoon	baking soda
teaspoon	salt

In a large mixing bowl, combine dry ingredients. Set aside.

cup plus 2 tablespoons	butter
cups	buttermilk
	eggs
teaspoons	vanilla

In another mixing bowl, melt butter. Add buttermilk, eggs, and vanilla. Whisk until combined. Pour liquid ingredients into dry ingredients. Whisk until smooth (batter will be thick). Pour ½ cup to ¾ cup of batter into very hot waffle iron. Bake until golden and crisp. Cool. Divide evenly among freezer bags. Seal bag, pressing out excess air. Freeze.

Granola

approximately 6 cups

1 cup	shredded coconut

Preheat oven to 350°. Spread coconut on a foil-lined baking tray. Toast 5 minutes. Stir. Toast 2 to 3 more minutes. Stir. Repeat as necessary until coconut is adequately toasted. Set aside.

4 cups	old-fashioned rolled oats
1 cup	nuts, chopped
¼ cup	sunflower seeds
2 tablespoons	wheat or oat bran
2 tablespoons	toasted wheat germ
1 tablespoon	sesame seeds
1 teaspoon	cinnamon
½ cup	butter, melted
½ cup	honey
1 teaspoon	vanilla
1 cup	dried fruit of choice

Reduce oven temperature to 300°. In a large mixing bowl, combine rolled oats, nuts, sunflower seeds, wheat or oat bran, wheat germ, sesame seeds, and cinnamon. Stir to combine. In a separate mixing bowl, stir together butter, honey, and vanilla. Pour over oat mixture. Stir to thoroughly combine. Divide between two foil-lined baking sheets. Toast in oven 30 minutes. Remove from oven. Cool. Break up granola pieces. Add toasted coconut and dried fruit. For long-term storage, portion as desired in freezer bags. Seal bags, pressing out excess air. Freeze.

Morning Glory Muffins

36 to 42 muffins

4 cups	all-purpose flour
2½ cups	sugar
4 teaspoons	baking soda
4 teaspoons	cinnamon
1 teaspoon	salt
4 cups	carrots, peeled and shredded
1 cup	raisins
1 cup	coconut
1 cup	pecans, chopped

Preheat oven to 350°. In a large mixing bowl, stir together all ingredients. Set aside.

6	eggs
2 cups	vegetable oil
2	apples, peeled and shredded
4 teaspoons	vanilla

In a large mixing bowl, whisk eggs. Whisk in all remaining ingredients. Pour over dry ingredients. Stir until thoroughly combined. Line muffin tins with paper cups. Fill each cup ⅔ full. Bake 20 minutes. Cool. Portion among freezer bags. Seal bag, pressing out excess air. Freeze.

Oven Omelet

(6) 5" x 7" or

(3) 5" x 12" or 8" x 8" or

(2) 9" x 13"

24	eggs
2 cups	milk
2 cups	half and half
2 teaspoons	salt
1 teaspoon	pepper

In a large bowl, beat eggs, milk, half and half, salt, and pepper until well blended. Add fresh, chopped herbs if desired.

2 cups	chopped, cooked meats, sautéed mushrooms and/or vegetables of choice

Consider using chopped cooked ham, bacon, sausage, or corned beef. Sauté or lightly steam onions, peppers, asparagus, zucchini, or broccoli. Diced tomatoes, drained, may be used fresh. Lightly sauté sliced mushrooms.

4 cups	shredded cheeses of choice

Preheat oven to 325°. Spray each tin with a nonstick cooking spray. Divide meats, mushrooms, and/or vegetables evenly among tins. Divide cheese evenly among tins. Top with egg mixture, dividing evenly among tins. Stir each tin gently to incorporate ingredients. Bake until omelets are set in the middle (approximately 35 to 45 minutes). Cool completely. Cover with a sheet of plastic wrap, pressing down to cling to food. Apply board lid. Freeze.

Reheating Instructions
Defrost in refrigerator. Remove board lid and plastic wrap. Transfer to saucepan or microwave safe dish and heat thoroughly.

Undoubtedly, omelets are best when they're fresh. But if having a frozen omelet on hand allows a break from cold cereal mornings, the compromise just may be worth it! Consider freezing oven omelets in individually-sized portions. They're ideal for hectic workdays and school days, and the high protein, low carb dieter!

Potato Sausage Bake

(6) 5" x 7" or

(3) 5" x 12" or 8" x 8" or

(2) 9" x 13"

pounds	breakfast sausage
cup	all-purpose flour
cups	milk
pounds	frozen, southern style hash brown potatoes
	green onions, finely chopped
cups	shredded sharp cheddar cheese

a large skillet over medium-high heat, brown sausage, breaking into small pieces
ith back of spoon. Drain. Return to pan. Sprinkle with flour and add in milk, stir-
ng until combined. Cook until mixture thickens and comes to boil, stirring occasion-
y (approximately 5 minutes). Spray each tin with nonstick cooking spray. Divide
ozen potatoes evenly among tins. Divide green onions, half of cheese, and sausage
enly among tins. Divide and sprinkle half of cheese over top of each tin. Cover with
sheet of plastic wrap, pressing down to cling to food. Apply board lid. Freeze.

aking Instructions

efrost in refrigerator. Preheat oven to 350°. Remove plastic wrap and board lid.
over loosely with foil. Bake until potatoes are tender (approximately 45 minutes).
rinkle with remaining green onions and serve.

Scrambled Egg and Cheese Biscuits

24 large biscuits

Biscuits

1	package dry yeast
¼ cup	lukewarm water
2 cups	buttermilk

In a small bowl, dissolve yeast in lukewarm water. Add buttermilk. Set aside.

5 cups	all-purpose flour
3 tablespoons	sugar
1 tablespoon	baking powder
1 teaspoon	baking soda
2 teaspoons	salt
¾ cup	vegetable shortening

Preheat oven to 425°. In a large mixing bowl, whisk together dry ingredients. Cut in vegetable shortening. Add buttermilk mixture, stirring to combine. Place on a lightly floured surface and knead briefly. Roll dough to ½-inch thickness, forming an even square. Using a pizza cutter, cut into an even grid of 25 square biscuits. Alternatively, cut with a biscuit cutter, rerolling dough until all is used. Place biscuits on a greased baking sheet. Cover and let rise 1 hour. Bake until lightly browned (approximately 8 minutes). Remove from oven. Set aside.

Scrambled Eggs

	butter
24	eggs
½ cup	water
	salt and pepper

In a large mixing bowl or pitcher, whisk together eggs and water. Work in batches as necessary. In a non-stick pan, melt enough butter to coat. Pour eggs into skillet. Over low heat, stir until eggs are firm but still moist. Remove from heat. Season with salt and pepper.

Assembling Biscuits

12 ounces	**cheese of preference, sliced**

Split each biscuit. Fill with scrambled eggs, topped with cheese. Wrap individually in foil. Portion as desired in freezer bags. Seal bag, pressing out excess air. Freeze.

Reheating Instructions

Defrost overnight in refrigerator. Preheat oven to 350°. Warm until heated through (approximately 20 minutes).

Breakfast-on-the-go doesn't get any easier than this! Consider varying your supply by adding sliced ham, bacon, or sausage. Add basil or chives to scrambled eggs. Use an unexpected cheese like Pepper Jack or Havarti with dill.

Marinades & Sauces

Cherry Barbecue Sauce
Teriyaki Sauce
Citrus Marinade
Five-Spice Marinade
Lemon Herb Marinade
Soy Sauce and Mango Chutney Marinade
Tandoori Marinade

Cherry Barbecue Sauce

approximately 4 cups

1¼ cups	apple cider vinegar
¾ cup	ketchup
¾ cup	chopped onion
¾ cup	dried cherries
⅓ cup	dark brown sugar, packed
¼ cup	water
¼ cup	molasses
2	large dried ancho chilies, stemmed and seeded
1 teaspoon	garlic, pressed or minced
1 teaspoon	ground coriander
	salt and pepper to taste

Prepare 1 cup barbecue sauce per 2-pound portion of boneless meat. In a heavy saucepan over medium heat, whisk together all ingredients. Bring to a boil. Reduce heat, cover, and simmer until chilies and cherries are tender (approximately 20 minutes). Cool. Working in batches, purée in blender. Return to saucepan and reduce, if desired. Cool. Season with salt and pepper. Package in freezer bags. Seal bag, pressing out excess air. Freeze.

Teriyaki Sauce

approximately 4 cups

2¼ cups	soy sauce
2¼ cups	brown sugar, packed
3 tablespoons	apple cider vinegar
2 tablespoons	vegetable oil
1 tablespoon	garlic, pressed or minced
1½ teaspoons	ground ginger

Prepare 1 cup marinade per 2-pound portion of boneless meat. In a saucepan over medium heat, whisk together all ingredients. Bring to a boil. Remove from heat. Cool. Package in freezer bags. Seal bag, pressing out excess air. Freeze.

Citrus Marinade

approximately 4 cups

1 cup	olive oil
¾ cup	fresh lemon juice
1 cup	fresh orange juice
6 tablespoons	balsamic vinegar
9 tablespoons	dark brown sugar, packed
4½ teaspoons	Dijon mustard
4½ teaspoons	lemon or orange zest
1½ teaspoons	garlic, pressed or minced

Prepare 1 cup marinade per 2-pound portion of boneless meat. In a medium bowl, whisk all ingredients until blended. Package in freezer bags. Seal bag, pressing out excess air. Freeze.

Preparing meals in advance doesn't get any easier than this! Place meat and marinade in a freezer bag (1 cup marinade per 2-pound portion of boneless meat). Freeze. To prepare, defrost overnight in refrigerator. Once defrosted, occasionally shake contents. Grill.

Five-Spice Marinade

approximately 4 cups

2	green onions (white and light green portion only), finely chopped
cup	dry Sherry
cup	soy sauce
cup	chili oil
cup	fresh ginger, minced
teaspoons	sesame oil
teaspoons	five-spice powder

Prepare 1 cup marinade per 2-pound portion of boneless meat. In a medium bowl, whisk all ingredients until blended. Package in freezer bags. Seal bag, pressing out excess air. Freeze.

Lemon Herb Marinade

approximately 3½ cups

¾ cup	olive oil
¾ cup	fresh lemon juice
2 tablespoons	garlic, pressed or minced
¾ cup	fresh parsley, coarsely chopped
¾ cup	fresh herbs of choice (basil, cilantro, dill, oregano, etc.), coarsely chopped
1½ teaspoons	hot pepper flakes
1½ teaspoons	cracked black pepper
1½ teaspoons	kosher salt
16 strips	lemon zest

Prepare 1 cup marinade per 2-pound portion of boneless meat. In a medium bowl, whisk all ingredients until blended. Package in freezer bags. Seal bag, pressing out excess air. Freeze.

You may wish to freeze some marinade separately so it may be served alongside grilled items. Place a portion in a separate freezer bag and attach it with a rubber band to the outside of the marinating bag.

Soy Sauce and Mango Chutney Marinade

approximately 4 cups

1½ cups	dry Sherry
¾ cup	soy sauce
¾ cup	sesame oil
¾ cup	mango chutney
6	green onions (white and light green portion only), finely chopped
5 tablespoons	honey
1½ tablespoons	fresh ginger, minced
1 tablespoon	garlic, pressed or minced
½ teaspoon	cayenne pepper

Prepare 1 cup marinade per 2-pound portion of boneless meat. In a medium bowl, whisk all ingredients until blended. Package in freezer bags. Seal bag, pressing out excess air. Freeze.

Tandoori Marinade

approximately 4 cups

4	medium onion, finely chopped
¾ cup	vegetable oil
½ cup	fresh lemon juice
¼ cup	fresh ginger, minced
2 tablespoons	ground coriander
4 teaspoons	garlic, pressed or minced
4 teaspoons	salt
4 teaspoons	ground cumin
2 teaspoons	tumeric
1 teaspoon	ground cardamom
1 teaspoon	cayenne pepper
1 cup	plain yogurt

Prepare 1 cup marinade per 2-pound portion of boneless meat. In a blender or food processor combine all ingredients except yogurt. Process until mixture becomes a thick paste. Pour in yogurt and process until just mixed. Package in freezer bags. Seal bag, pressing out excess air. Freeze.

Dry Mixes

Bacon Dip Mix
Breading Mix
Buttermilk Pancake Mix
Cornmeal Biscuit Mix
Hot Cocoa Mix
Ranch Dressing Mix
Savory Biscuit Mix
Seasoned Salt
Taco Seasoning Mix
Vegetable Dip Mix

Bacon Dip Mix

approximately 1 cup

½ cup plus 2 tablespoons	instant bacon bits
5 tablespoons	dried minced onion
5 teaspoons	instant beef bouillon
1 tablespoon	dried minced garlic

In a small bowl, combine all ingredients, mixing well. Place in an airtight container. Store in a cool, dry place.

Preparation Instructions

Stir or shake well before using. In a small bowl, combine 3 tablespoons Bacon Dip Mix with 1 cup of sour cream. Stir to thoroughly combine. Cover and refrigerate at least 1 hour before serving. Serve with assorted crackers. Yogurt or softened cream cheese may be substituted for sour cream.

Breading Mix

approximately 1 cup

1 cup	plain breadcrumbs
½ teaspoon	salt
½ teaspoon	dried parsley
¼ teaspoon	garlic powder
¼ teaspoon	onion powder
¼ teaspoon	sugar
dash	oregano

In a small bowl, combine all ingredients, mixing well. Place in an airtight container. Store in a cool, dry place.

Preparation Instructions

Stir or shake well before using. Use as an Italian-style breading when frying or baking chicken, fish, pork chops, eggplant, etc.

Buttermilk Pancake Mix

approximately 10 cups

cups	dry buttermilk powder
cups	all-purpose flour
cup	sugar
teaspoons	baking powder
teaspoons	baking soda
teaspoons	salt

a large bowl, combine all ingredients, mixing well. Place in an airtight container.
tore in the refrigerator.

Preparation Instructions

tir or shake well before using. In a mixing bowl, combine 1½ cups Buttermilk
ancake Mix, 1 egg, 2 tablespoons vegetable oil, and 1 cup water (more as needed).
tir until just mixed (mixture will be lumpy). Let stand 5 minutes. Lightly oil a large
riddle or skillet and heat over medium heat. Pour approximately 3 tablespoons batter
er pancake into skillet. Cook pancakes for 1½ to 2 minutes (or when large bubbles
orm on the uncooked surface) and flip, cooking 30 more seconds. Serve immediately
r keep warm on a baking sheet in a 200° oven until all pancakes are prepared. Makes
pproximately 10 pancakes.

With some creative packaging, dry mixes can become wonderful gifts and would be ideal for housewarmings, showers, teacher appreciation, welcoming a new neighbor, or thanking a hostess.

Cornmeal Biscuit Mix

24 biscuits

4½ cups	all-purpose flour
1 cup plus 2 tablespoons	yellow cornmeal
2 tablespoons	baking powder
2¼ teaspoons	baking soda
2¼ teaspoons	salt
4½ tablespoons	sugar
1 cup plus 2 tablespoons	butter, chilled and cut into ½-inch pieces

Work in batches of no more than 24 biscuits. In a large bowl or processor, stir together
all dry ingredients. Cut in butter using a pastry knife, fork, or processor. For each 4
biscuit serving, package and freeze 1⅓ cups dry mix in each freezer bag. Seal bag, pressing out excess air. Freeze.

Baking Instructions

Preheat oven to 450°. Bring mix to room temperature and place in bowl. For each 4
biscuit serving, add 6 tablespoons buttermilk. Stir gently until mixture holds together.
On a lightly floured surface, pat into a square, approximately 1-inch thick. Cut into
squares. Place on a baking sheet and bake until golden (approximately 15 minutes).

Hot Cocoa Mix

approximately 15 cups (45 servings)

10 cups	powdered dry milk
5 cups	powdered sugar
2 cups	unsweetened cocoa powder
8 ounces	powdered non-dairy creamer (flavor of choice)

In a large bowl, combine all ingredients, mixing well. Place in an airtight container. Store in a cool, dry place.

Preparation Instructions

Stir or shake well before using. Place ⅓ cup Hot Cocoa Mix in a coffee cup or mug. Add ¾ cup boiling water. Stir to dissolve. Top with whipped cream or marshmallows, if desired.

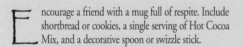

Encourage a friend with a mug full of respite. Include shortbread or cookies, a single serving of Hot Cocoa Mix, and a decorative spoon or swizzle stick.

Ranch Dressing Mix

approximately 3 cups

1 cup	dried parsley
½ cup	saltines, finely crushed (about 15 crackers)
½ cup	dried minced onion
½ cup	garlic salt
½ cup	onion salt
¼ cup	garlic powder
¼ cup	onion powder
2 tablespoons	dill weed

In a large bowl, combine all ingredients, mixing well. Place in an airtight container. Store in a cool, dry place.

Preparation Instructions

Ranch Dressing

Stir or shake well before using. In a small bowl, combine 2 tablespoons Ranch Dressing Mix with 2 cups of mayonnaise and 2 cups of buttermilk. Stir thoroughly to combine. Cover and refrigerate. Makes 4 cups.

Thousand Island Dressing

Add ¼ cup chili sauce and 2 tablespoons pickle relish to 1 cup prepared Ranch Dressing.

Cucumber Dressing

Add 1 medium cucumber (peeled, seeded, and minced) and 1 teaspoon celery seed to 1 cup prepared Ranch Dressing.

Savory Biscuit Mix

24 biscuits

cups	all-purpose flour
tablespoons	baking powder
tablespoons	dried chives
tablespoon	dried dill
tablespoon	sugar
½ teaspoons	salt
½ teaspoons	ground black pepper
teaspoon	paprika
cup plus 2 ablespoons	butter, chilled

Vork in batches of no more than 24 biscuits. In a large bowl or processor, stir together ll dry ingredients. Cut in butter using a pastry knife, fork, or processor. For each 4 iscuit serving, package and freeze 1⅓ cups dry mix in each freezer bag. Seal bag, press-ng out excess air. Freeze.

Baking Instructions

reheat oven to 450º. Bring mix to room temperature and place in bowl. For each 4 iscuit serving, add 6 tablespoons half and half. Stir gently until mixture forms a ball.)n a lightly floured surface, pat into a square, approximately ¾-inch thick. Cut into quares. Place on a baking sheet and bake until golden (approximately 15 minutes).

Seasoned Salt

approximately 1 cup

¼ cup	salt
1 tablespoon	dried parsley
1 tablespoon	dried minced onion
1 tablespoon	ground black pepper
1 tablespoon	instant chicken bouillon
1 tablespoon	garlic salt
1 tablespoon	chili powder
1 teaspoon	onion salt
1 teaspoon	onion powder
1 teaspoon	cumin powder
1 teaspoon	dried marjoram
1 teaspoon	paprika
½ teaspoon	curry powder

In a small bowl, combine all ingredients, mixing well. Place in an airtight container. Store in a cool, dry place. Stir or shake well before using.

Taco Seasoning Mix

approximately 1 cup

5 tablespoons	chili powder
3 tablespoons	onion powder
5 teaspoons	ground cumin
5 teaspoons	garlic powder
5 teaspoons	paprika
5 teaspoons	dried oregano
5 teaspoons	salt
2 teaspoons	sugar

In a small bowl, combine all ingredients, mixing well. Place in an airtight container. Store in a cool, dry place.

Preparation Instructions

Stir or shake well before using. Add ¼ cup Taco Seasoning Mix and 1 cup water to 1 to 1½ pounds browned ground beef. Simmer 15 minutes.

Vegetable Dip Mix

approximately ¾ cup

¼ cup	dried parsley
¼ cup	dried thyme
2 tablespoons	dried tarragon
2 tablespoons	dried minced onion
1 tablespoon	garlic powder
½ teaspoon	salt
½ teaspoon	black pepper., coarsely ground

In a small bowl, combine all ingredients, mixing well. Place in an airtight container. Store in a cool, dry place.

Preparation Instructions

Stir or shake well to combine. In a small bowl, combine 1 tablespoon Vegetable Dip Mix, ¾ cup sour cream, ¼ cup mayonnaise, and 1 teaspoon lemon juice. Stir thoroughly to combine. Cover and refrigerate at least 4 hours before serving. Serve with assorted fresh vegetables.

À la Carte

Green Beans in Sour Cream
Herbed Stuffing
Puréed Carrots with Ginger
Rice Pilaf
Scalloped Potatoes
Southern Sweet Potato Bake

Green Beans in Sour Cream

(6) 5" x 7" or

(3) 5" x 12" or 8" x 8" or

(2) 9" x 13"

2 tablespoons	butter
1 cup	dry breadcrumbs

In a small bowl, melt butter in microwave. Stir in breadcrumbs until thoroughly coated with butter. Set aside.

3 pounds	frozen, French-cut green beans
¼ cup	butter
2	small onions, finely chopped
¼ cup	all-purpose flour
2 teaspoons	dried parsley
2 teaspoons	salt
½ teaspoon	ground black pepper
1 pound	sour cream
2 tablespoons	dry sherry
2 cups	shredded cheddar cheese

Cook green beans according to package directions. Set aside. In a skillet over medium heat, melt butter. Sauté onion 5 minutes. Stir in flour, parsley, salt, pepper, sour cream, and sherry and cook 3 minutes. Add beans, stirring until mixture is evenly combined. Spray each tin with nonstick cooking spray. Divide bean mixture evenly among tins. Divide cheese and then breadcrumbs evenly among tins. Cover with a sheet of plastic wrap, pressing down to cling to food. Apply board lid. Freeze.

Baking Instructions

Defrost in refrigerator. Preheat oven to 350°. Remove board lid and plastic wrap. Bake until heated through (approximately 30 minutes).

Herbed Stuffing

24 servings

3 pounds	crusty country style bread, cut into ½-inch cubes

Preheat oven to 325°. Work in batches as necessary. Spread bread cubes on cookie sheets. Toast in oven until dry (approximately 30 minutes). Stir midway during toasting for even browning.

1½ cups	butter
8	medium onions, finely chopped
8	celery ribs, finely chopped

Work in batches as necessary. In a large skillet over medium heat, melt butter. Sauté onions and celery until tender. Remove from heat and set aside.

1 tablespoon	dried thyme
1½ teaspoons	dried sage
1½ teaspoons	dried rosemary
6 cups	chicken stock or canned broth
	salt and pepper to taste

In a large bowl, place toasted bread cubes, sautéed vegetables, dried herbs, and chicken stock or canned broth, stirring until evenly combined. Season with salt and pepper. Divide evenly among tins. Cover with a sheet of plastic wrap, pressing down to cling to food. Apply board lid. Freeze.

Baking Instructions

Defrost in refrigerator. Preheat oven to 350°. Remove board lid and plastic wrap. Cover loosely with foil to prevent drying. Bake until heated through and lightly browned (approximately 25 to 30 minutes).

Add interest and flavor to stuffing with intriguing ingredients like sautéed mushrooms, cooked, chopped bacon, chopped nuts (pecans, walnuts, hazelnuts), chopped fresh fruit (apples, pears), or chopped dried fruit (cherries, cranberries, apricots, raisins, currants).

Puréed Carrots with Ginger

(6) 5" x 7" or

(3) 5" x 12" or 8" x 8" or

(2) 9" x 13"

pounds	carrots
cup	sugar
tablespoon	salt

el carrots. Chop carrots in food processor using a 1/2-inch, or approximate, blade. ce carrots, sugar and salt in a large stockpot. Cover with water. Bring to a boil over dium-high heat. Reduce to low and simmer until tender (approximately 45 min- es). Drain. Set aside.

cups	fresh orange juice
cups	butter, softened
cup plus 2	fresh ginger, minced
blespoons	
tablespoons	orange zest
tablespoons	fresh lemon juice
tablespoons	sugar

a heavy saucepan over medium heat, bring orange juice to simmer. Add butter, gin- , and orange zest. Stir until butter melts. Remove from heat and stir in lemon juice d sugar. Work in batches as necessary. Purée carrots with juice mixture until ooth. Transfer to a large bowl and stir thoroughly to harmonize batches. Divide nly among tins. Cool. Cover with a sheet of plastic wrap, pressing down to cling to d. Apply board lid. Freeze.

eheating Instructions

frost in refrigerator. Remove board lid and plastic wrap. Transfer to saucepan or crowave safe dish and heat thoroughly (stirring frequently over medium-low heat if ng stovetop).

Rice Pilaf

24 servings

¾ cup	olive or vegetable oil
¾ cup	butter
6 cups	rice
2	medium onions, chopped
1 tablespoon	garlic, pressed or minced
13½ cups	chicken stock or canned broth
2 tablespoons	dried thyme
2 teaspoons	dried basil
1½ teaspoons	dried marjoram

Work in batches as necessary. In a large skillet over medium-high heat, heat oil and butter. Add rice, onion, and garlic and sauté until lightly browned. Stir in chicken stock or canned broth, thyme, basil, and marjoram. Bring to a boil. Reduce heat, cover, and simmer until liquid is absorbed and rice is tender (approximately 25 minutes.) Divide evenly among tins. Cover with a sheet of plastic wrap, pressing down to cling to food. Apply board lid. Freeze.

Reheating Instructions

Defrost in refrigerator. Remove board lid and plastic wrap. Transfer to a microwave safe dish and heat thoroughly.

Scalloped Potatoes

(6) 5" x 7" or

(3) 5" x 12" or 8" x 8" or

(2) 9" x 13"

10 pounds	potatoes, peeled and sliced ⅛-inch thick

In a large stockpot, bring salted water to boil. Add potatoes. Return to boil, reduce heat, and simmer until potatoes are softened, yet firm (approximately 15 to 20 minutes). Drain potatoes. Set aside.

1 cup	butter
1	medium onion, finely chopped
1 cup	all-purpose flour
6 cups	milk, scalded
2 cups	chicken stock or canned broth
8 cups	shredded sharp cheddar cheese
¾ cup	breadcrumbs
	salt and pepper to taste

Work in batches as necessary. In a large stockpot over medium heat, melt butter. Sauté onions until tender. Stir in flour and cook 3 to 5 minutes. Slowly add scalded milk and chicken stock or canned broth, whisking to combine. Continue whisking over medium heat until thickened. Remove from heat. Stir in cheese until melted. Season with salt and pepper. Divide half of potatoes evenly among tins. Divide half of cheese sauce evenly among tins. Repeat. Divide and sprinkle breadcrumbs evenly among tins. Cool. Cover with a sheet of plastic wrap, pressing down to cling to food. Apply board lid. Freeze.

Reheating Instructions

Defrost in refrigerator. Preheat oven to 350°. Remove board lid and plastic wrap. Cover loosely with foil to halt browning if necessary. Bake until potatoes are tender (approximately 40 minutes).

> If you find that potatoes frequently sprout before being consumed in your home, consider preparing and freezing a large quantity of potatoes in various forms. Frozen twice-baked potatoes, mashed potatoes, and scalloped potatoes reheat beautifully.

Southern Sweet Potato Bake

(6) 5" x 7" or

(3) 5" x 12" or 8" x 8" or

(2) 9" x 13"

10 pounds	sweet potatoes

Preheat oven to 350°. Bake sweet potatoes on a foil-lined baking sheet until tender (approximately 1½ hours). Cool, peel, and place in a large mixing bowl.

1 cup	butter, softened
1⅓ cups	sugar
1 cup	brown sugar, packed
1 cup	honey
1 tablespoon	vanilla
2 teaspoons	salt
1 teaspoon	cinnamon
1 teaspoon	nutmeg
6	eggs
2 cups	milk

Work in batches as necessary. Add butter, sugars, honey, and vanilla to warm sweet potatoes. Beat on medium speed until smooth. Add salt, cinnamon, and nutmeg. Beat in eggs. Slowly add milk, beating to combine. Divide sweet potato mixture evenly among tins.

1 cup	butter, chilled
2 cups	all-purpose flour
2 cups	brown sugar, packed
1 teaspoon	cinnamon
1 teaspoon	nutmeg
½ teaspoon	salt
2 cups	pecans, chopped

Using a pastry knife or food processor, cut butter into flour, sugar, cinnamon, nutmeg, and salt. Stir in pecans. Cover sweet potatoes with topping, dividing evenly among tins. Cover with a sheet of plastic wrap, pressing down to cling to food. Apply board lid. Freeze.

Reheating Instructions

Defrost in refrigerator. Preheat oven to 375°. Remove board lid and plastic wrap. Cover loosely with foil to halt browning if necessary. Bake until browned and cooked through (approximately 1 hour).

Chapter 6

Freezing—A Quick Review

Freezing—A Quick Review

Packaging

The quality of your meal will be dependent upon the quality of your packaging materials. While *Cookin[g] Among Friends*® is designed to use frozen foods quickly, it is still best to package foods as if intended for long[-] term freezer storage. Choose materials that are moisture-proof and seal in such a way that excludes as much a[ir] as possible. The materials used should be nonporous to prevent flavors and odors from entering or leaving an[d] should have no taste or odor of their own. They should be easy to seal and label. Freezer plastic wrap, aluminu[m] foil, freezer bags, and aluminum tins with board lids are wonderful choices.

To prevent freezer burn, eliminate as much air contact with food as possible. When filling freezer bag[s] squeeze out air before sealing. When using aluminum tins with board lids (our personal favorite), seal off foo[d] from the air by placing a layer of freezer plastic wrap over the food, pressing down to cling, and thereby helpin[g] to form an air-proof and moisture-proof barrier.

If you wish to avoid purchasing disposable/recyclable packaging, consider lining various containers wit[h] heavy-duty aluminum foil or freezer plastic wrap, filling, sealing, and freezing. After freezing, the food an[d] wrapping can be removed from the container and restacked for more efficient use of space.

Our Favorite Packaging - The Aluminum Tin with Board Lid

After experimenting with bags, foils and wraps, we discovered the aluminum tin with board lid. It [has] become the mainstay of our packaging line-up. We love that it's so easy to fill. It stacks beautifully in the freez[er] and optimizes storage space. It protects food well. It's attractive. It can go straight into the oven and into man[y] new microwaves. It's cost effective. And it's recyclable.

Tins may be available in bulk at your local warehouse outlet or food service outlet. Dividing a case amon[g] your group makes the aluminum tin a very reasonable packaging option. A wonderful assortment of sizes, [at] favorable prices, is also available from *Cooking Among Friends, LLC.* Contact us at our mailing address, ema[il] address, website, or by phone.

Labeling

Label all food items before they are frozen. Labels can be prepared and applied to packaging materials we[ll] before your final cooking period. Include the name of the entrée, date prepared, and any special instructions f[or] reheating and serving. You can use a permanent marker, such as a Sharpie®, to write directly on freezer bag[s] board lids, and aluminum foil. Like applying labels, you will need to do this before the entrée is frozen. Labe[ls] and ink do not adhere well to frozen surfaces.

Meal Management

You may wish to prepare and maintain a list of items that are in your freezer. See our form, *Keeping All Together*. This form can be completed at each exchange, indicating the items that will be taken home or storage in the freezer and perhaps even in the pantry. As items are used, quantities are "counted down."

Freezing

To preserve food quality and ensure food safety you will want to cool and freeze your entrées as rapidly as possible. Refrigerate entrées quickly after their preparation. After thoroughly cooling, freeze.

To promote rapid freezing, you may wish to lower your freezer's temperature by 10° 24 hours before freezing your meals. Add the amount of unfrozen food to your freezer that will freeze within a 24-hour time period (approximately 2 to 3 pounds of food for each cubic foot of freezer capacity). Scatter meals throughout your freezer. After the meals are frozen, you can then stack them to most efficiently use space and maintain organization.

Thawing

It is best to thoroughly defrost your entrée before baking or reheating. For good food safety, thaw entrées in the refrigerator (not on the counter). You can also thaw packaged meals in a cold-water bath, changing the water frequently. Frozen foods can be removed from the packaging, placed in a microwave safe dish, and defrosted in the microwave. Once an entrée is defrosted, we do not recommend refreezing.

What Freezes Well . . . and What Doesn't

The freezing process does change food. The trick to a successful experience with *Cooking Among Friends*® is choosing recipes that freeze well–those that are minimally affected by the freezing process. We have found that it pays to experiment! While many freezer references forbid the freezing of sour cream, for example, we have found that in many recipes where it is suspended in a sauce, it freezes beautifully. Or, at worst, some diligent stirring (or adding a bit of fresh sour cream) is required during the reheating process. So don't be afraid to try a family-favorite recipe containing a questionable ingredient by freezing a portion, defrosting, and reheating for a quality test. Some foods definitely do not freeze well. Avoid freezing mayonnaise, sour cream (unless suspended in a sauce), eggs in a shell, lettuce and other greens, cucumbers, radishes, and raw celery.

Take a strategic approach to preparing food items for freezing. Keep in mind that cooked items will have the opportunity to soak up additional liquid, and that they'll be subjected to reheating. Slightly undercook pasta and potatoes. Cook rice until just tender. Cook vegetables until tender crisp.

Chapter 7

Resources

Cooking Among Friends®

Quantity Equivalents

Container Sizes:
8 x 8 x 1½ = 6 cups = 1½ quarts
9 x 9 x 1½ = 8 cups = 2 quarts
11 x 7 x 1½ = 8 cups = 2 quarts
13 x 9 x 2 = 14 cups = 3½ quarts

Measurements:
1 teaspoon = ⅓ tablespoon
1 tablespoon = 3 teaspoons = ½ ounce liquid and dry
2 tablespoons = 1 ounce
4 tablespoons = 2 ounces = ¼ cup
8 tablespoons = 4 ounces = ½ cup
12 tablespoons = 6 ounces = ¾ cup
16 tablespoons = 8 ounces = 1 cup = ½ pound
32 tablespoons = 16 ounces = 2 cups = 1 pound
64 tablespoons = 32 ounces = 1 quart = 2 pounds
¼ cup = 4 tablespoons
⅜ cup = ¼ cup plus 2 tablespoons
⅝ cup = ¼ cup plus 2 tablespoons
⅞ cup = ¾ cup plus 2 tablespoons
1 cup = 8 ounces (liquid) = ½ pint
2 cups = 16 ounces (liquid) = 1 pint
4 cups = 32 ounces (liquid) = 2 pints = 1 quart
8 cups = 64 ounces (liquid) = 2 quarts
16 cups = 128 ounces (liquid) = 4 quarts = 1 gallon

Contents of Cans:
No. 1 tall = 2 cups
No. 2 (18 - 20 oz) = 2½ cups
No. 2½ (26 - 30 oz) = 3½ cups
No. 3 (32 oz) = 4 cups
No. 5 (4 lbs - 4¼ lbs) = 8 cups
No. 10 (6 lbs - 7 lbs) = 11½ to 13 cups
No. 300 (14 - 16 oz)= 1¾ cups
No. 303 (1 lb) = 2 cups

One No. 10 can is approximately equivalent to:

   7 No. 303 (1 lb) cans
   5 No. 2 (18 - 20 oz) cans
   4 No. 2½ (26 - 30 oz) cans

Fruit:
1 medium apple = 1 cup chopped
3 medium apples = 1 pound
3 medium bananas = 1½ cups mashed
1 lemon = approximately 3 tablespoons lemon juice
1 lemon rind = 1 - 1½ teaspoons lemon zest
1 lime = approximately 2 tablespoons lime juice
1 lime rind = 1 teaspoon lime zest
1 orange = approximately 6 - 8 tablespoons orange juice
1 orange rind = 2 - 3 tablespoons orange zest

Vegetables:
3 ounces button mushrooms raw, sliced = 1 cup
1 pound button mushrooms raw, sliced = 4 cups
6 ounces canned button mushrooms = ½ pound fresh
1 pound carrots = 6 - 7 medium carrots = 3 cups chopped
4 large celery ribs = 1 cup chopped or diced
1 medium green pepper, chopped = about 1 cup
1 medium onion, chopped = about 1 cup
3 medium potatoes = 1 pound = 2 cups cubed
2 pounds sauerkraut = about 2¾ cups
1 medium tomato = 1 cup chopped
8-ounce can tomato sauce = 14 tablespoons (1 cup minus 2 tablespoons)
14.5-ounce can diced tomatoes = 1¾ cups
14.5-ounce can stewed tomatoes = 1¾ cups
14.5-ounce can whole tomatoes = 1¾ cups
28-ounce can crushed tomatoes = 3 cups
28-ounce can diced tomatoes = 3½ cups
28-ounce can whole tomatoes = 3½ cups
29-ounce can tomato sauce = 3¼ cups
12-ounce can tomato paste = 22 tablespoons
8 14.5-ounce cans diced tomato, undrained = 116 ounces = about 14 cups
No. 10 (6 lb 7 oz) can diced tomatoes = approximately 12 cups

Spices:
-inch piece of ginger, minced = 1 tablespoon
clove garlic = ½ teaspoon minced fresh garlic
10 cloves garlic = 5 teaspoons
30 cloves garlic = 5 tablespoons

Meat:
2 pounds beef cut into 1" chunks = about 15 cups raw
pounds beef cut into 1" chunks = about 10 cups raw
pounds beef cut into 1" chunks = about 5 cups raw
pound beef chunks cooked = about 2 cups
pound ground beef, browned = about 2 cups
pound cooked, chopped chicken breast = about 2 cups
pound boneless, skinless chicken = 4 4-ounce
breasts
pound bone-in turkey breast = about 6 cups
chunked meat
- 8 pound turkey = 7 - 8 cups chunked meat
- 4 pound chicken = about 4 cups cooked meat

Dry Goods/Grains:
pound all purpose flour = 4 cups
pound granulated sugar = 2¼ - 2½ cups
pound confectioner's sugar = 3¾ - 4 cups
pound brown sugar = 2¼ cups, packed
pound yellow cornmeal = 2⅔ cups
pound uncooked oatmeal = 5 cups
cup uncooked long-grain rice = 3 - 4 cups cooked
pound uncooked long-grain rice = 10 cups cooked
cup uncooked quick-cooking rice = 2 cups cooked
ounces pearl barley = 1 cup uncooked
ounces rice/bulgar wheat/millet/wheat = 1 cup
uncooked
ounces semolina/ground rice/tapioca = 1 cup
uncooked
slice fresh bread with crust = ½ cup crumbs
ounces dried breadcrumbs = 1 cup
pound loaf bread = 12 - 16 slices

Pasta/Legumes:
cup (4 ounces) uncooked macaroni = 2¼ cups
cooked
pound spaghetti uncooked = 5 - 6 cups cooked
cup (4 ounces) dry egg noodles = 2 - 3 cups cooked
pound dry egg noodles = 9 cups cooked
ounces dried beans = 1 cup

1 pound dried beans = 2½ cups = 6 cups cooked
1 pound dried lentils = 2¼ cups = 5 cups cooked
2 pounds dried white northern beans = 12 cups
cooked
6 lbs. - 12 oz. great northern beans (No. 10) =
about 12 cups

Fats/Cheeses/Dairy:
1 ounce butter, margarine, oil = 2 tablespoons
8 ounces butter, margarine, oil = 1 cup
1 pound butter = 4 sticks = 2 cups = 32 tablespoons
4 ounces shredded cheddar cheese = 1 cup
3 ounces shredded Parmesan cheese = 1 cup
1 pound grated cheese = 4 - 5 cups
1 pound shredded mozzarella cheese = 4 cups
1 pound sour cream = approximately 1¾ cups
9 ounces sour cream = approximately 1 cup
14-ounce can evaporated milk = 1¼ cups
1 large egg = 2 ounces = ¼ cup = 4 tablespoons
1 egg yolk = 1 tablespoon + 1 teaspoon
1 egg white = 2 tablespoons + 2 teaspoons

Dried Fruit/Nuts/Etc:
5-6 ounces currants/raisins, chopped candied peel =
1 cup
1 pound raisins = 2¾ cup
1 pound chopped, pitted dates = 2½ cups
12 ounce bag whole cranberries = 2¾ cups chopped
= 3 cups whole
8 ounces peanut butter = 1 cup
5 ounces whole shelled almonds = 1 cup
5 ounces slivered almonds = 1 cup
4 ounces flaked coconut = 1⅓ cups
1 pound chopped walnuts = 4 cups
1 pound chopped pecans = 4 cups
6 ounces chocolate chips = 1 cup
14 squares graham crackers = 1 cup crumbs

Preserves/Sweeteners:
10 ounces red currant jelly = 1 cup
12 ounces clear honey/golden syrup = 1 cup
11 ounces maple/corn syrup = 1 cup
11 ounces molasses = 1 cup
5-6 ounces jam/marmalade/jelly = ½ cup

Cooking Among Friends®
Establishing Group Guidelines

Consider this our "wish list." Each of our potential group members will complete his or her own form. Doing so will provide us with lots of great information and help us determine our compatibility as a group. We'll discuss our surveys together, arrive at consensus, and compile our official guidelines. Bypass anything that stumps you (we'll discuss it later), and check all that apply.

Quantity and Frequency

Our group will optimally be comprised of ___ members. Each member will provide at least ___ entrées to every other member once every _____ (frequency).

Entrée Size

For each exchange gathering, entrées will be brought packaged, labeled, and frozen. Our optimal entrée size will be:

		Add-a-Side Entrée	Stand-Alone Entrée
_____	2 person serving	2 cups	3 cups
_____	4 person serving	4 cups	6 cups
_____	6 person serving	6 cups	9 cups
_____	8 person serving	8 cups	12 cups

An Add-a-Side Entrée is a meaty or hearty item intended to be served with or over an additional side. Examples include Beef Stroganoff (to be served over noodles or mashed potatoes), Chicken Parmigiana (to be served with side items of your choosing), and Hunan Chicken (to be served over rice).

A Stand-Alone Entrée is an item inclusive of rice, pasta, or significant amounts of sauce or vegetables (soups and stews). While you may wish to add side items when serving this item, it is not necessary for the completion of the dish. Examples include Lasagna, White Chicken Chili and Turkey Pot Pie.

Finance

_____ We commit to be savvy shoppers.

_____ We feel that everyone should spend approximately the same amount of money to prepare his or her entrée. Therefore we will establish a per exchange budgetary figure. This figure serves as our target. While we commit to provide a minimum number of meals with this target in mind, savvy shopping or inexpensive-to-prepare recipes may make it possible to provide an additional portion for the group. (For example, a member preparing Lentil Chili will be obligated to provide the number of meals that the budgetary figure allows, which would be more portions than a member preparing a meat dish.) If our expenses exceed the budgetary guideline, we understand that the difference will not be adjusted or refunded by the group. Our financial guideline will be $_____ per exchange.

_____ We will not attempt to maintain financial equality. We concur that members may spend as little or as much as is necessary to prepare the minimum quantity of entrées we have established.

The Exchange Gathering

Our *Cooking Among Friends*® group can most easily meet on a _____ (day) at _____ (time of day). At this meeting, we will exchange our frozen entrées, determine the upcoming menu, decide who will prepare what items, and set the date and location for the next exchange. Members are encouraged to be on the lookout for delicious, freezer-friendly recipes, and to bring them to the exchange gathering.

Because we want our group experience to get better and better, we'll poll last exchange's recipes to determine whether or not they will be prepared again in the future.

_____ Our exchange gatherings will be brief and "business only."

_____ We consider our exchange gatherings to be a wonderful chance to not only swap our meals and to prepare for next time, but to visit and have some fun together!

_____ We will take turns planning and hosting the exchange gathering.

_____ Yikes! Let's evaluate our meals privately using the *Cooking Among Friends*® evaluation form. Completed forms will be handed in to our group's facilitator. Receiving repeated "single star" ratings (indicating a lack of consideration for the established group guidelines) will be an indication that a member is not a good match for the group.

_____ We'll bravely indicate whether an entrée is eligible for repetition at the exchange gathering. We'll use the phrase, "My husband/the kids/the neighbors didn't care for it."

Beyond Entrées

_____ We commit to preparing entrées for exchange on a regular basis. Additionally, each time we meet to exchange entrées and to establish the next menu, any member of the group may propose the exchange of additional items. While no one is expected to join in the exchange of additional items, this will be a way to add flexibility and creativity to our group. Any one, or all, may wish to join in the exchange of supplemental baked goods, breakfast items, etc., as described in *Going Beyond Entrées*.

Preparing entrées will be the primary focus of our group. However, I am intrigued by the following exchange possibilities!

_____ Baked Goods		_____ Party Foods
_____ Desserts		_____ Cookie Dough
_____ Soup's On!		_____ Breakfast
_____ The Holiday Meal		_____ Ice Cream
_____ The Farmer's Market		_____ Marinades
_____ Staples Stock-Up		_____ Culinary TLC
_____ The Mini-Exchange		_____ Gifts from the Pantry

_____	Dry Mixes	_____	Kid Pleasers
_____	More Mileage from a Single Entrée	_____	À la Carte

Packaging

_____ Let's investigate purchasing bulk packaging materials as offered by *Cooking Among Friends, LLC* and elsewhere.

Diet Restrictions

As a group, we recognize that we may not be able to serve everyone's needs. We realize that those with severe or multiple diet restrictions would be best served by a *Cooking Among Friends®* group where all or most members have similar restrictions. We will seek to find common elements among our members. Our group has agreed to choose recipes that do not contain the following items:

_____ Meat
_____ Wheat products
_____ Dairy products
_____ Eggs
_____ Shellfish
_____ Peanuts
_____ MSG
_____ Alcohol
_____ Aspartame (NutraSweet, Equal, Sweet & Low)
_____ Other _____

Preferences

We realize that we will be most successful as a group if we are able to meet the expectations of one another. While we do not wish to cook with ingredients that might be distasteful to some, too many restrictions will greatly limit the recipes we'll be able to prepare. If, for example, mushrooms aren't preferred by just a few, but can be tolerated, they should not be excluded. Our preference guidelines have been established in a balanced way to optimize quality and taste and are indicated below.

Fat Content

_____ No fat
_____ Low fat
_____ No preference

Sodium

_____ Low sodium
_____ Well, but not overly, salted

Seasoning

_____ Mild (will add seasoning later as desired)
_____ Medium
_____ Spicy
_____ No preference

Prepared Sauces and Soups

_____ Prefer homemade
_____ No preference
_____ Exceptions _____

Packaged Foods

_____ Packaged foods (meat "helper" products, "instant" products) not acceptable
_____ Packaged foods (meat "helper" products, "instant" products) acceptable
_____ Exceptions _____

Poultry

_____ White meat only
_____ Dark meat only
_____ Mixed white and dark meat
_____ No preference
_____ Deboned poultry should always be carefully removed of skin, gristle and fat

Ground Beef

_____ Ground sirloin or better (99% lean)
_____ Ground round or better (85% lean)
_____ Ground chuck or better (78% lean)
_____ No preference (hamburger acceptable)

Meat

_____ All meat should be carefully removed of gristle and fat

Produce

_____ Use only fresh produce
_____ Use fresh or frozen produce (fresh preferred)
_____ Use fresh, frozen, or canned produce (fresh or frozen preferred)
_____ Exceptions _____

Grains

	Whole grains preferred
_____	Whole grains preferred
_____	Processed grains preferred
_____	No preference

Meat/Produce/Grains

_____	Range fed/natural/organic only
_____	Range fed/natural/organic preferred but not necessary
_____	Range fed/natural/organic unnecessary

Brands

_____	Name brands only
_____	Generic or store brands acceptable
_____	Exceptions _____

Pasta Preparation (for sauces to be served over pasta)

_____ Pasta will be provided separately for each member of the group.
_____ We will consider pasta a staple item and each member will purchase the pasta of their choice.

Rice Preparation (for sauces to be served over rice)

_____ Rice will be provided separately for each member of the group.
_____ We will consider rice a staple item and each member will purchase the rice of their choice.

Additional preferences or dislikes _____

_____

_____

Concerns I'd like to discuss as a group_____

_____

_____

Cooking Among Friends, LLC
P.O. Box 84
Allendale, Michigan 49401

616.895.6909   www.cookingamongfriends.com   mailbox@cookingamongfriends.com

Cooking Among Friends®
Official Group Guidelines

ntity and Frequency

Our group will optimally be comprised of ___ members. Each member will provide at least ___ entrées to every other member once every _____ (frequency).

rée Size

For each exchange gathering, entrées will be brought packaged, labeled, and frozen. Our optimal entrée size will be:

		Add-a-Side Entrée	Stand-Alone Entrée
_____	2 person serving	2 cups	3 cups
_____	4 person serving	4 cups	6 cups
_____	6 person serving	6 cups	9 cups
_____	8 person serving	8 cups	12 cups

An Add-a-Side Entrée is a meaty or hearty item intended to be served with or over an additional side. Examples include Beef Stroganoff (to be served over noodles or mashed potatoes), Chicken Parmigiana (to be served with side items of your choosing), and Hunan Chicken (to be served over rice).

A Stand-Alone Entrée is an item inclusive of rice, pasta, or significant amounts of sauce or vegetables (soups and stews). While you may wish to add side items when serving this item, it is not necessary for the completion of the dish. Examples include Lasagna, White Chicken Chili and Turkey Pot Pie.

nce

_____ We commit to be savvy shoppers.

_____ We feel that everyone should spend approximately the same amount of money to prepare his or her entrée. Therefore we will establish a per exchange budgetary figure. This figure serves as our target. While we commit to provide a minimum number of meals with this target in mind, savvy shopping or inexpensive-to-prepare recipes may make it possible to provide an additional portion for the group. (For example, a member preparing Lentil Chili will be obligated to provide the number of meals that the budgetary figure allows, which would be more portions than a member preparing a meat dish.) If our expenses exceed the budgetary guideline, we understand that the difference will not be adjusted or refunded by the group. Our financial guideline will be $_____ per exchange.

_____   We will not attempt to maintain financial equality. We concur that members may spend as little or as much as is necessary to prepare the minimum quantity of entrées we have established.

The Exchange Gathering

Our *Cooking Among Friends*® group can most easily meet on a _____ (day) at _____ (time of day). At this meeting, we will exchange our frozen entrées, determine the upcoming menu, decide who will prepare what items, and set the date and location for the next exchange. Members are encouraged to be on the lookout for delicious, freezer-friendly recipes, and to bring them to the exchange gathering.

Because we want our group experience to get better and better, we'll poll last exchange's recipes to determine whether or not they will be prepared again in the future.

_____   Our exchange gatherings will be brief and "business only."

_____   We consider our exchange gatherings to be a wonderful chance to not only swap our meals and to prepare for next time, but to visit and have some fun together!

_____   We will take turns planning and hosting the exchange gathering.

_____   Yikes! Let's evaluate our meals privately using the *Cooking Among Friends*® evaluation form. Completed forms will be handed in to our group's facilitator. Receiving repeated "single star" ratings (indicating a lack of consideration for the established group guidelines) will be an indication that a member is not a good match for the group.

_____   We'll bravely indicate whether an entrée is eligible for repetition at the exchange gathering. We'll use the phrase, "My husband/the kids/the neighbors didn't care for it."

Beyond Entrées

_____   We commit to preparing entrées for exchange on a regular basis. Additionally, each time we meet to exchange entrées and to establish the next menu, any member of the group may propose the exchange of additional items. While no one is expected to join in the exchange of additional items, this will be a way to add flexibility and creativity to our group. Any one, or all, may wish to join in the exchange of supplemental baked goods, breakfast items, etc., as described in *Going Beyond Entrées*.

_____ Preparing entrées will be the primary focus of our group. However, members of our group have expressed interest in the following exchange possibilities!

_____	Baked Goods	_____	Party Foods
_____	Desserts	_____	Cookie Dough
_____	Soup's On!	_____	Breakfast
_____	The Holiday Meal	_____	Ice Cream
_____	The Farmer's Market	_____	Marinades
_____	Staples Stock-Up	_____	Culinary TLC

_____ The Mini-Exchange
_____ Dry Mixes
_____ More Mileage from
a Single Entrée

_____ Gifts from the Pantry
_____ Kid Pleasers
_____ À la Carte

Diet Restrictions

As a group, we recognize that we may not be able to serve everyone's needs. We realize that those with severe or multiple diet restrictions would be best served by a *Cooking Among Friends*® group where all or most members have similar restrictions. We will seek to find common elements among our members. Our group has agreed to choose recipes that do not contain the following items:

_____ Meat
_____ Wheat products
_____ Dairy products
_____ Eggs
_____ Shellfish
_____ Peanuts
_____ MSG
_____ Alcohol
_____ Aspartame (NutraSweet, Equal, Sweet & Low)
_____ Other _____

Preferences

We realize that we will be most successful as a group if we are able to meet the expectations of one another. While we do not wish to cook with ingredients that might be distasteful to some, too many restrictions will greatly limit the recipes we'll be able to prepare. If, for example, mushrooms aren't preferred by just a few, but can be tolerated, they should not be excluded. Our preference guidelines have been established in a balanced way to optimize quality and taste and are indicated below.

Fat Content
_____ No fat
_____ Low fat
_____ No preference

Sodium
_____ Low sodium
_____ Well, but not overly, salted

Seasoning

_____	Mild (will add seasoning later as desired)
_____	Medium
_____	Spicy
_____	No preference

Prepared Sauces and Soups

_____	Prefer homemade
_____	No preference
_____	Exceptions _____

Packaged Foods

_____	Packaged foods (meat "helper" products, "instant" products) not acceptable
_____	Packaged foods (meat "helper" products, "instant" products) acceptable
_____	Exceptions _____

Poultry

_____	White meat only
_____	Dark meat only
_____	Mixed white and dark meat
_____	No preference
_____	Deboned poultry should always be carefully removed of skin, gristle and fat

Ground Beef

_____	Ground sirloin or better (99% lean)
_____	Ground round or better (85% lean)
_____	Ground chuck or better (78% lean)
_____	No preference (hamburger acceptable)

Meat

_____	All meat should be carefully removed of gristle and fat

Produce

_____	Use only fresh produce
_____	Use fresh or frozen produce (fresh preferred)
_____	Use fresh, frozen, or canned produce (fresh or frozen preferred)
_____	Exceptions _____

Grains

_____ Whole grains preferred
_____ Processed grains preferred
_____ No preference

Meat/Produce/Grains

_____ Range fed/natural/organic only
_____ Range fed/natural/organic preferred but not necessary
_____ Range fed/natural/organic unnecessary

Brands

_____ Name brands only
_____ Generic or store brands acceptable
_____ Exceptions _____

Pasta Preparation (for sauces to be served over pasta)

_____ Pasta will be provided separately for each member of the group.
_____ We will consider pasta a staple item and each member will purchase the pasta of their choice.

Rice Preparation (for sauces to be served over rice)

_____ Rice will be provided separately for each member of the group.
_____ will consider rice a staple item and each member will purchase the rice of their choice.

Additional preferences or dislikes _____

_____

_____

Cooking Among Friends®

Favorite Exchange Recipes

Chicken	Beef	Ground Beef
_____	_____	_____
_____	_____	_____
_____	_____	_____
_____	_____	_____
_____	_____	_____
_____	_____	_____
_____	_____	_____
_____	_____	_____
_____	_____	_____
_____	_____	_____
_____	_____	_____
_____	_____	_____
_____	_____	_____
_____	_____	_____
_____	_____	_____
_____	_____	_____
_____	_____	_____
_____	_____	_____
_____	_____	_____
_____	_____	_____
_____	_____	_____

Soups-n-Stews

_____
_____
_____
_____
_____
_____
_____
_____
_____
_____
_____
_____

Turkey

_____
_____
_____
_____
_____
_____
_____
_____
_____
_____
_____

Seafood

_____
_____
_____
_____
_____
_____
_____
_____
_____
_____
_____

Meatless

_____
_____
_____
_____
_____
_____
_____
_____
_____
_____
_____
_____

Pork

_____
_____
_____
_____
_____
_____
_____
_____
_____
_____

Other

_____
_____
_____
_____
_____
_____
_____
_____
_____
_____
_____

Cooking Among Friends®
Keeping It All Together

Exchange Date _____ Time _____ Location _____

Menu Plan					Entrée Inventory			Entrée Evaluati
Preparer	Qty	Beyond Entrées	Qty	Entrées	Inventory Countdown	Accompaniments in the Pantry	Supplemental Shopping List	★★★ ★★ / ★★★

Notes

★★★★★
Make it again!

★★★
Let's continue t
search for the per
recipe.

★
This did not me
our Official Gro
Guidelines.

Form supplies are available directly from *Cooking Among Friends, LLC.* Contact us at our mailing address, email address, website, or by phone.